Welcome to the United States
A Guide for New Immigrants

 U.S. Citizenship
and Immigration
Services

U.S. GOVERNMENT OFFICIAL EDITION NOTICE

This is the Official U.S. Government edition of this publication and is herein identified to certify its authenticity. Use of the ISBN 978-0-16-092967-0 is for U.S. Government Publishing Office Official Editions only. The Superintendent of Documents of the U.S. Government Publishing Office requests that any reprinted edition clearly be labeled as a copy of the authentic work with a new ISBN.

The information presented in *Welcome to the United States: A Guide for New Immigrants* is considered public information and may be distributed or copied without alteration unless otherwise specified. The citation should be:

U.S. Department of Homeland Security, U.S. Citizenship and Immigration Services, Office of Citizenship, *Welcome to the United States: A Guide for New Immigrants*, Washington, DC, 2015.

U.S. Citizenship and Immigration Services (USCIS) has purchased the right to use many of the images in *Welcome to the United States: A Guide for New Immigrants*. USCIS is licensed to use these images on a non-exclusive and non-transferable basis. All other rights to the images, including without limitation and copyright, are retained by the owner of the images. These images are not in the public domain and may not be used except as they appear as part of this guide.

This guide contains information on a variety of topics that are not within the jurisdiction of U.S. Department of Homeland Security (DHS)/USCIS. If you have a question about a non-DHS/USCIS issue, please refer directly to the responsible agency or organization for the most current information. This information is correct at the time of printing, however, it may change in the future.

For sale by the Superintendent of Documents, U.S. Government Publishing Office
Internet: bookstore.gpo.gov Phone: toll free (866) 512-1800; DC area (202) 512-1800
Fax: (202) 512-2104 Mail: Stop IDCC, Washington, DC 20402-0001

ISBN 978-0-16-092967-0

Table of Contents

Welcome to the United States
A Guide for New Immigrants

Congratulations on becoming a permanent resident of the United States of America! On behalf of the president of the United States and the American people, we welcome you and wish you every success here.

The United States has a long history of welcoming immigrants from all parts of the world. America values the contributions of immigrants who continue to enrich this country and preserve its legacy as a land of freedom and opportunity.

As a permanent resident of the United States, you have made a decision to call this country your home. As you work to achieve your goals, take time to get to know this country, its history, and its people. It is now both your right and your responsibility to shape the future of the United States and to ensure its continued success.

Exciting opportunities await you as you begin your life as a permanent resident of this great country. Welcome to the United States!

U.S. Citizenship and Immigration Services

Federal Departments and Agencies

If you have a question and do not know which department can answer it, call 1-800-FED-INFO (or 1-800-333-4636). If you are hearing impaired, call 1-800-326-2996.

You can also visit **www.usa.gov** for general information about federal departments and agencies.

U.S. Department of Education (ED)

Phone: 1-800-USA-LEARN
Phone: 1-800-872-5327
For hearing impaired: 1-800-437-0833
www.ed.gov

U.S. Equal Employment Opportunity Commission (EEOC)

Phone: 1-800-669-4000
For hearing impaired: 1-800-669-6820
www.eeoc.gov

U.S. Department of Health and Human Services (HHS)

Phone: 1-877-696-6775
www.hhs.gov

U.S. Department of Homeland Security (DHS)

Phone: 202-282-8000
www.dhs.gov

U.S. Citizenship and Immigration Services (USCIS)

Phone: 1-800-375-5283
For hearing impaired: 1-800-767-1833
www.uscis.gov

U.S. Customs and Border Protection (CBP)

Phone: 202-354-1000
www.cbp.gov

U.S. Immigration and Customs Enforcement (ICE)

www.ice.gov

U.S. Department of Housing and Urban Development (HUD)

Phone: 202-708-1112
For hearing impaired: 202-708-1455
www.hud.gov

U.S. Department of Justice (DOJ)

Phone: 202-514-2000
www.justice.gov

U.S. Department of the Treasury

Internal Revenue Service (IRS)
Phone: 1-800-829-1040
For hearing impaired: 1-800-829-4059
www.irs.gov

Selective Service System (SSS)

Phone: 1-888-655-1825
Phone: 847-688-6888
For hearing impaired: 847-688-2567
www.sss.gov

Social Security Administration (SSA)

Phone: 1-800-772-1213
For hearing impaired: 1-800-325-0778
www.socialsecurity.gov or **www.segurosocial.gov/espanol**

U.S. Department of State (DOS)

Phone: 202-647-4000
For hearing impaired: 1-800-877-8339
www.state.gov

The United States Today

The United States also includes the territories of Guam, American Samoa, the U.S. Virgin Islands, and the commonwealths of the Northern Mariana Islands and Puerto Rico, which do not appear on this map.

Federal Holidays

Most federal offices are closed on official holidays. If a holiday falls on a Saturday, it is observed on the preceding Friday. If a holiday falls on a Sunday, it is observed on the following Monday. Many non-government employers also give their employees a holiday on these days. The federal government observes the following official holidays.

New Year's Day	January 1
Birthday of Martin Luther King, Jr.	3rd Monday in January
Presidents' Day	3rd Monday in February
Memorial Day	Last Monday in May
Independence Day	July 4
Labor Day	1st Monday in September
Columbus Day	2nd Monday in October
Veterans Day	November 11
Thanksgiving Day	4th Thursday in November
Christmas Day	December 25

Contact USCIS

Visit the USCIS website at **www.uscis.gov** and **www.welcometousa.gov**, a resource for new immigrants.

Call Customer Service at 1-800-375-5283 or 1-800-767-1833 (for hearing impaired).

To get forms, visit the USCIS website or call the USCIS Forms Line at 1-800-870-3676.

About This Guide

This guide contains basic information to help you settle in the United States and find what you and your family need for everyday life. It also summarizes important information about your legal status and about agencies and organizations that provide documents or essential services you may need.

As a permanent resident, you should begin to learn about this country, its people, and its system of government. Use this guide to find out about your rights and responsibilities as an immigrant and to understand how federal, state, and local governments work. You can also learn about important historical events that have shaped the United States, as well as the importance of getting involved in your community and suggestions on how to do so.

This guide provides a general summary of rights, responsibilities, and procedures related to permanent residents. To get more specific and detailed information, you should consult the laws, regulations, forms, and guidance of U.S. Citizenship and Immigration Services (USCIS). You should always consult these more detailed resources for your specific immigration question or case. You can find this information on the USCIS website at **www.uscis.gov**. You can obtain USCIS forms on the website or by calling the USCIS Forms Line at 1-800-870-3676. For more information, call Customer Service at 1-800-375-5283 or 1-800-767-1833 (for hearing impaired).

Where to Get Help

This guide will help you get started, but it cannot answer all the questions you might have about life in the United States. For additional information, you can contact a state, county, or city government office to learn about available services or consult with local organizations that help new immigrants. You can find these offices and organizations by using the free resources described below.

The Public Library

Public libraries in the United States are free and open to everyone. Libraries are located in almost every community. The library staff can help you find information on many topics and can give you a library card that allows you to borrow items, such as books, DVDs, and other resources, free of charge. Most libraries also have local newspapers for you to read and computers that you can use to access the Internet.

Some libraries offer free computer classes, English language instruction, and other programs for children and adults. Ask the library staff about the services offered in your community. To find a library near you, visit **www.nces.ed.gov**.

The Phone Book

Your local phone book (telephone directory) contains phone numbers and important information about federal, state, and local community services. The phone book has emergency information, local maps, and information about how to get phone service. The white pages list phone numbers of individuals and the yellow pages list phone numbers and addresses for businesses and organizations. You can also dial 411 on your phone to get a specific phone number anywhere in the United States. You may have to pay a fee when calling 411.

The Internet

The Internet can link you to many sources of information, including the websites of federal, state, and local government agencies. Most government websites end with ".gov." If you do not have a computer at home, you can use one in your public library. You can use the Internet to search for jobs, find housing, learn about schools, and locate community organizations and resources to help you. You can also use the Internet to learn about important news and current events, and to discover interesting information about life in America, U.S. history and government, and your local community. To locate federal government resources available to new immigrants, visit **www. welcometousa.gov**.

TIP

As an immigrant, you should be aware that dishonest people have made fake websites that look like government websites to confuse you and take advantage of you. Remember, the official website of U.S. Citizenship and Immigration Services is **www.uscis.gov**.

Community and Faith-Based Organizations That Assist Immigrants

There are organizations in many communities that provide free or very low-cost assistance to immigrants. These organizations can help you learn about your community and the services available to you as an immigrant. You can find these organizations by searching the Internet, looking in your local phone book, asking the staff at the public library, or by contacting your local government social service agency.

USCIS Online Resources

USCIS has a variety of helpful online resources available. These resources provide information about immigration topics, processing times, case status, fees, and other benefits.

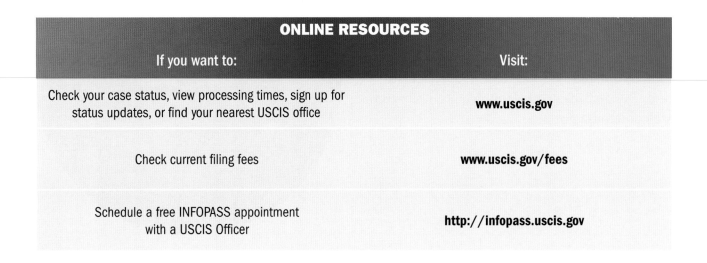

ONLINE RESOURCES	
If you want to:	**Visit:**
Check your case status, view processing times, sign up for status updates, or find your nearest USCIS office	**www.uscis.gov**
Check current filing fees	**www.uscis.gov/fees**
Schedule a free INFOPASS appointment with a USCIS Officer	**http://infopass.uscis.gov**

More Information for New Immigrants

Welcome to the United States: A Guide for New Immigrants is available in additional languages at **www.uscis.gov/newimmigrants**.

Your Rights and Responsibilities as a Permanent Resident

As a permanent resident, you are expected to consider the United States your home and to respect and obey this country's laws. Being a permanent resident also means that you have new rights and responsibilities.

Being a permanent resident is a privilege, not a right. The U.S. government can take away your permanent resident status under certain conditions. You must maintain your permanent resident status if you want to live and work in the United States and become a citizen one day.

In this section, you will learn what it means to be a permanent resident and what you need to do to maintain your permanent resident status.

Your Rights and Responsibilities

Your conduct as a permanent resident can affect your ability to become a U.S. citizen later. The process of becoming a U.S. citizen is called naturalization.

As a permanent resident, you have the right to:

- Live permanently anywhere in the United States.

- Work in the United States.

- Own property in the United States.

- Attend public school.

- Apply for a driver's license in your state or territory.

- Join certain branches of the U.S. armed forces.

- Receive Social Security, Supplemental Security Income, and Medicare benefits, if you are eligible.

- Apply to become a U.S. citizen once you are eligible.

- Request visas for your spouse and unmarried children to live in the United States.

- Leave and return to the United States under certain conditions.

As a permanent resident, you must:

- Obey all federal, state, and local laws.

- Pay federal, state, and local income taxes.

- Register with the Selective Service (U.S. armed forces), if you are a male between the ages of 18 and 26. See page 18 for instructions.

- Maintain your immigration status.

- Carry proof of your permanent resident status at all times.

- Change your address online or provide it in writing to USCIS within 10 days of each time you move. See page 19 for instructions.

What You Can Do

As a permanent resident, you have many rights and freedoms. In return, you have some responsibilities. One important responsibility is to get involved in your community. You should also learn about American culture, history, and government. You can do this by taking adult education classes and reading local newspapers.

Permanent residents are issued a valid Permanent Resident Card (Form I-551) as proof of their legal status in the United States. Some people call this a "Green Card." If you are immigrating to the United States and will be admitted as a permanent resident, you must pay the USCIS immigrant fee. You pay this fee online through the USCIS Electronic Immigration System (USCIS ELIS) at **www.uscis.gov/uscis-elis**. Please note that you will not receive your Permanent Resident Card until you have paid the USCIS immigrant fee. If you became a permanent resident by adjusting your status while you were in the United States, you pay only the Form I-485, Application to Register Permanent Residence or Adjust Status, filing fee and not the USCIS immigrant fee.

If you are a permanent resident who is 18 years old or older, you must carry proof of your immigration status. You must show it to an immigration officer or law enforcement officer if asked for it. Your Permanent Resident Card can be valid for 10 years, and you must renew it before it expires or if your name changes. To replace or renew your Permanent Resident Card, you must file Form I-90, Application to Replace Permanent Resident Card. There is a fee to file Form I-90. You can get this form online at **www.uscis.gov** or by calling the USCIS Forms Line at 1-800-870-3676. If you are a conditional permanent resident (CR) through marriage or entrepreneurship, you were issued a two-year card. Do not use Form I-90 to apply for an extension or renewal of your status. Instead, you must file for removal of your conditions before your card expires. See page 19 for instructions on how to remove the conditions on your permanent resident status.

Your Permanent Resident Card shows that you are allowed to live and work in the United States. You can also use your Permanent Resident Card to re-enter the United States after traveling abroad. If you are outside of the United States for more than 12 months, then you will need to show additional documentation to re-enter the country as a permanent resident. For more information on these documents, see page 17.

Maintaining Your Permanent Resident Status

Once you have obtained permanent resident status, you will continue to be a permanent resident unless your status changes as provided under U.S. immigration law. One way you can lose permanent resident status is by abandoning it. You abandon your permanent resident status by leaving the United States to live abroad permanently with the intent of giving up your permanent resident status. Your conduct will demonstrate your actual intent. There are some things you can do to decrease the possibility that the U.S. government will find that you have abandoned your status:

- Do not leave the United States for an extended period of time unless the circumstances show that your trip is for a temporary purpose (for example, to attend school, take a temporary job, or care for a family member). If you are absent for a year or longer, you cannot use your Permanent Resident Card to enter the United States.

- If something happens that delays your return, be prepared to explain the reason(s) for the delay.

- File federal and, if applicable, state, and local income tax returns.

- Register with the Selective Service if you are a male between the ages of 18 and 26.

- Give your new address to USCIS within 10 days of each time you move.

Safeguard Important Documents

Keep important documents that you brought from your home country in a safe place. Examples of important documents include: a passport, birth certificate, marriage certificate, divorce certificate, diplomas showing that you have graduated from high school or college, and/or certificates that show you have special training or skills.

Keep Your Immigration Status

Some immigrants believe they can live abroad and keep their permanent resident status as long as they return to the United States at least once a year, but this assumption is incorrect. Travel to the United States once a year may not be sufficient to maintain your status. Permanent residents may travel outside the United States, and temporary or brief travel usually does not affect your permanent resident status. If you leave the country for too long or indicate in another way that you do not intend to make the United States your permanent home, the U.S. government may determine that you have abandoned your permanent resident status. This can also occur if you take a trip that is between six months and a year, if there is evidence that you did not intend to make the United States your permanent home.

You can use your Permanent Resident Card as a travel document for returning to the United States if you have not been abroad for a year or more. If you think you will be out of the United States for more than 12 months, you should apply for a re-entry permit **before** leaving the country by filing Form I-131, Application for a Travel Document. You must pay a fee to file Form I-131. You can get Form I-131 at **www.uscis.gov** or by calling the USCIS Forms Line at 1-800-870-3676.

A re-entry permit is valid for up to two years. At a port of entry, you may show the re-entry permit instead of a visa or Permanent Resident Card. Having a re-entry permit does not guarantee that you will be admitted to the United States when you return, but it can make it easier to show that you are returning from a temporary visit abroad. If you would like additional information about international travel as a permanent resident, please visit **www.uscis.gov**.

You should also be aware that—regardless of whether you might have abandoned your permanent resident status—you are subject to a full immigration inspection as an applicant for admission any time you have been abroad for at least 181 days, or in other situations specified in immigration law.

File Tax Returns

As a permanent resident, you must file income tax returns and report your income to the Internal Revenue Service (IRS) as well as to your state, city, or local tax department, if required. If you do not file income tax returns while living outside of the United States for any length of time, or if you say that you are a non-immigrant on your tax returns, the U.S. government may decide that you have given up your permanent resident status.

Register with the Selective Service

All men between the ages of 18 and 26 years old must register with the Selective Service. Males who obtained their immigrant visa or adjusted their status at that age may have automatically been registered with the Selective Service. If so, you should have received information in the mail stating that you are registered. If you are unsure if you are registered, speak with someone from the Selective Service who can check your record. You can also check on the Selective Service website at **www.sss.gov**. When you register, you tell the government that you are available to serve in the U.S. armed forces. The United States does not have a military draft now, but men between the ages of 18 and 26 are still required to register. Unless they want to, permanent residents and U.S. citizens do not have to serve in the armed forces.

You can register at a U.S. post office or on the Internet. To register for Selective Service on the Internet, visit the Selective Service System at **www.sss.gov**. To speak with someone from the Selective Service, call 847-688-6888. This is not a free call.

You can also find information on the USCIS website at **www.uscis.gov**.

Give Your New Address to USCIS

You must notify USCIS if you change your address. File Form AR-11, Change of Address, within 10 days of your relocation. For information on filing a change of address, go to the USCIS website at **www.uscis.gov/addresschange** or call Customer Service at 1-800-375-5283. You must notify USCIS **each time** you change your address.

For more information, call USCIS at 1-800-375-5283 or visit **www.uscis.gov**.

If You Are a Conditional Permanent Resident

You may be in the United States as a conditional permanent resident (CR). You are a CR if you were married for less than two years to your U.S. citizen or permanent resident spouse on the day your permanent resident status was granted. If you have children, they also may be CRs. See Form I-751, Petition to Remove the Conditions on Residence, for instructions on the filing process for children. Some immigrant investors are also CRs.

A CR has the same rights and responsibilities as a permanent resident. Conditional permanent residents must file Form I-751, and immigrant investors must file Form I-829, Petition by Entrepreneur to Remove Conditions, **within** two years of the date they were granted conditional permanent resident status. This date is usually the expiration date of your Permanent Resident Card. You should file these forms **within** the 90-day period **prior** to the two-year anniversary of when you got your conditional permanent residence. If you do not do this, you could lose your immigration status.

Filing Form I-751 with Your Husband or Wife

If you are a CR and you immigrated based on your marriage to a U.S. citizen or permanent resident, then you and your spouse must file Form I-751 together so that you can remove the conditions on your permanent resident status.

Sometimes, you do not have to file Form I-751 with your husband or wife. If you are no longer married to your spouse or if your spouse abused you, you can file Form I-751 by yourself. You can also file Form I-751 by yourself if deportation from the United States would result in extreme hardship. If you are not applying with your spouse, you can file Form I-751 at any time after you become a CR.

Filing USCIS Forms I-751 and I-829

Who: Conditional permanent resident (CR)

Why: Conditional permanent resident status expires two years **after** the date you became a CR.

When: Conditional permanent resident filing together with his or her spouse must file Form I-751. Immigrant investors must file Form I-829. Both of these forms must be filed within the 90 days **before** conditional permanent residence status expires. The expiration date is on your Permanent Resident Card.

Where to get the form: You can get the form at **www.uscis.gov** or by calling the USCIS Forms Line at 1-800-870-3676.

Where to send the form: Send it to a USCIS service center. The addresses of the service centers are in the instructions for the form.

What it costs: You must pay a fee to file Form I-751 or Form I-829. Before you submit the form, check for the most current USCIS filing fees at **www.uscis.gov/fees**.

If you file Form I-751 or Form I-829 on time, USCIS will usually send you a notice extending your CR status for up to 12 months. During this time, USCIS will review your application.

If You Are a Victim of Domestic Abuse

If you are a victim of domestic abuse, you can find help through the National Domestic Violence Hotline at 1-800-799-7233 or 1-800-787-3224 (for hearing impaired). Help is available in Spanish and other languages.

The Violence Against Women Act allows abused spouses and children of U.S. citizens and permanent residents to self-petition, or file their own petition, to become a permanent resident. See **www.uscis.gov** or call the National Domestic Violence Hotline for more information.

Keep several copies of all forms you send to USCIS and other government offices. Send copies, not originals. Sometimes forms get lost, so keeping copies can help avoid problems.

Finding Legal Assistance

If you need help with an immigration issue, you can use the services of a licensed immigration lawyer. You can check with your local bar association for help finding a qualified lawyer.

Some states certify specialists in immigration law. These attorneys have passed tests to prove that they have special knowledge about immigration law. The following states currently list certified specialists on their state bar websites: California, Florida, North Carolina, and Texas. Note: You are responsible for determining whether to hire an attorney. USCIS does not endorse or recommend any particular attorney.

If you need legal help on an immigration issue but do not have enough money to hire a lawyer, there are some low-cost or free assistance options. Consider asking for assistance from one of the following places:

- **A Recognized Organization:** Organizations that are recognized by the Board of Immigration Appeals (BIA). For an organization to be recognized, it must have enough knowledge and experience to provide services to immigrants. A recognized organization can charge or accept only very small fees for those services. For a list of these BIA-recognized organizations, visit **www.justice.gov/eoir/recognition-accreditation-roster-reports**.

- **An Accredited Representative:** People who are connected to BIA-recognized organizations. These representatives can charge or accept only very small fees for their services. For a list of these BIA-accredited representatives, visit **www.justice.gov/eoir/recognition-accreditation-roster-reports**.

- **A Qualified Representative:** People who will provide free services. These representatives must know about immigration law and the rules of practice in court. Law school students and graduates, and people with good moral character who have a personal or professional affiliation with you (relative, neighbor, clergy, co-worker, or friend) are all examples of qualified representatives.

- **Free Legal Service Providers:** The Department of Justice has a list of recognized free legal service providers for people who are in immigration proceedings. This is a list of attorneys and organizations that may be willing to represent immigrants in proceedings before immigration courts. The attorneys and organizations on this list have agreed to help immigrants pro bono (free of charge) only in immigration proceedings. Some of them may not be able to help you with non-court-related matters, such as visa petitions, naturalization, etc. The list is available at **www.justice.gov/eoir/free-legal-services-providers**.

- **Pro Bono Program:** Local lists of recognized pro bono organizations and their representatives are usually available at each local USCIS office.

For more information about finding legal services, please visit **www.uscis.gov/legaladvice**.

Beware of Immigration Fraud

Many immigration practitioners are well qualified and honest, and they can provide good services to immigrants, however, there are some people who take advantage of immigrants.

Before you decide to get help with immigration matters and before you pay any money, you should do research so you can make the right decision about what kind of legal help you need. Protect yourself from becoming a victim of immigration fraud.

Important things to remember:

- No private organization or person offering help with immigration issues has a special connection with USCIS. Ask questions of people who make promises that sound too good to be true or who claim to have a special relationship with USCIS. Do not trust people who guarantee results or faster processing. If you are not eligible for an immigration benefit, using an immigration lawyer or consultant will not change that fact.

- Some consultants, travel agencies, real estate offices, and people called "notaries public" offer immigration services. Be sure to ask questions about their qualifications and ask to see copies of their BIA accreditation letter or bar certificate. Some people who say they are qualified to offer legal services are not. These people can make mistakes that could put your immigration status at risk and cause serious problems for you.

- If you use an immigration consultant or lawyer, get a written contract. The contract should be in both English and in your native language (if English is not your native language). The contract should list all services that will be provided to you and how much they will cost. Ask for references before you sign the contract.

- Try to avoid paying cash for services. Make sure you get a receipt for your payment. Be sure to keep your original documents.

- Never sign a blank form or application. Make sure you understand what you are signing.

For more information about how to protect yourself from becoming a victim of immigration fraud, visit **www.uscis.gov/avoidscams**.

Get help if an immigration consultant has cheated you. Call your state or local district attorney, consumer affairs department, or local police department. You can also contact the Federal Trade Commission to report the unauthorized practice of immigration law by visiting **www.ftccomplaintassistant.gov**.

Consequences of Criminal Behavior for Permanent Residents

The United States is a law-abiding society. Permanent residents in the United States must obey all laws. If you are a permanent resident and engage in or are convicted of a crime in the United States, you could have serious problems. You could be removed from the country, refused re-entry into the United States if you leave the country, lose your permanent resident status, and, in certain circumstances, lose your eligibility for U.S. citizenship.

Examples of crimes that may affect your permanent resident status include:

- A crime defined as an aggravated felony, which includes crimes of violence that are felonies with a one-year prison term;

- Murder;

- Rape;

- Sexual assault against a child;

- Illegal trafficking in drugs, firearms, or people; and

- A crime of moral turpitude, which, in general, is a crime with an intent to steal or defraud, a crime where physical harm is done or threatened, a crime where serious physical harm is caused by reckless behavior, or a crime of sexual misconduct.

There are also serious consequences for you as a permanent resident if you:

- Lie to get immigration benefits for yourself or someone else;

- Say you are a U.S. citizen if you are not;

- Vote in a federal election or in a state or local election open only to U.S. citizens;

- Are a habitual drunkard or someone who is drunk or uses illegal drugs most of the time;

- Are married to more than one person at the same time;

- Fail to support your family or to pay child or spousal support as ordered;

- Are arrested for domestic violence (domestic violence is when someone assaults or harasses a family member, which includes violating a protection order);

- Lie or present fake documents to get public benefits or defraud any government agency;

- Fail to file tax returns when required;

- Willfully fail to register for the Selective Service if you are a male between the ages of 18 and 26; and

- Help someone else who is not a U.S. citizen or national to enter the United States illegally even if that person is a close relative and you are not paid.

If you have committed or have been convicted of a crime, you should consult with a reputable immigration lawyer or a community-based organization that provides legal service to immigrants before you apply for another immigration benefit. See page 21 for information on how to find legal assistance.

Getting Settled in the United States

This section provides information that can help you adjust to life in the United States. You will learn how to get a Social Security number, find a place to live, look for a job, find child care, and travel in the United States.

Get a Social Security Number

As a permanent resident, you are eligible for a Social Security number, which is a number assigned to you by the U.S. government. It helps the government keep track of your earnings and the benefits you can receive. Your Social Security number is also used by financial institutions and other agencies, such as schools, to identify you. You may be asked for your Social Security number when you rent an apartment or buy a home.

Social Security is a U.S. government program that provides benefits for certain retired workers and their families, certain disabled workers and their families, and certain family members of deceased workers. The government department in charge of Social Security is called the Social Security Administration (SSA).

Find the Social Security office closest to you by:

- Looking on the SSA website, **www.socialsecurity.gov**. For Spanish, visit **www.segurosocial.gov/espanol**. The website also has limited information available in several other languages.

- Calling 1-800-772-1213 or 1-800-325-0778 (for hearing impaired) between 7 a.m. and 7 p.m. Free interpreter services are available.

If You Do Not Speak English

The Social Security office can provide an interpreter free of charge to help you apply for a Social Security number. When you call the Social Security office, tell the person who answers the phone that you do not speak English. They will find an interpreter to help. You can also get assistance from an interpreter when you visit the Social Security office.

The Social Security Administration website contains helpful information for people new to the United States. The "Other Languages" section of the website has information about Social Security in several languages. Visit **www.socialsecurity.gov**; for Spanish, see **www.segurosocial.gov/espanol**.

You do **not** need to fill out an application or go to a Social Security office to get a Social Security number if **all** of the following conditions apply to you:

- You asked for a Social Security number or card when you applied for an immigrant visa;

- You applied for an immigrant visa in October 2002 or later; and

- You were 18 years old or older when you came to the United States.

In this situation, the Departments of State and Homeland Security sent the required information to assign you a Social Security number to the Social Security Administration (SSA). The SSA will assign you a Social Security number and mail your Social Security card to the same U.S. mailing address where USCIS sends your Permanent Resident Card. You should get your Social Security card within three weeks after you arrive in the United States. If you do not receive your card within three weeks after arriving in the United States, contact the SSA immediately. Also, contact the SSA if you change your mailing address **after** you arrive but **before** you receive your Social Security card.

You **must** go to a Social Security office to get a Social Security number if **any** of the following conditions apply to you:

- You did not ask for a Social Security number or card when you applied for an immigrant visa;

- You applied for your immigrant visa before October 2002; or

- You were under age 18 when you came to the United States.

A Social Security representative will help you apply for a Social Security number. Bring the following documents with you when you go to the Social Security office to apply:

- A birth certificate or other document, such as your passport, showing when and where you were born.

- A document showing your immigration status, including your permission to work in the United States. This can be your Permanent Resident Card or passport with an immigration stamp or visa label.

The SSA will send your Social Security number to you in the mail. You should receive your Social Security card about two weeks after the SSA has all documents needed for your application. If SSA needs to verify any of your documents, it may take longer to receive your Social Security number.

Find a Place to Live

You can choose where you live in the United States. Many people stay with friends or family members when they first arrive. Others move into their own housing.

In the United States, most people spend about 25 percent of their income on housing. Here are some housing options you may consider.

Renting a Home

Apartments and houses can be rented. You can find these in several ways:

- Look for "Apartment Available" or "For Rent" signs on buildings.

- Ask friends, relatives, and co-workers if they know of places to rent.

- Look for "For Rent" signs in public spaces, such as bulletin boards in your library, grocery stores, and community centers.

- Research places available for rent on the Internet. If you do not have a computer at home, you can use one at your local public library.

- Look in the phone book's yellow pages under "Property Management." These are companies that rent apartments and houses. They may charge you a fee to help you find a home.

- Look in the "Classifieds" section of the newspaper. Find the pages listing "Apartments for Rent" and "Homes for Rent." These will have information about renting homes and apartments.

- Call a local real estate agent.

Call 311 for Information on City or Town Services

In many cities and towns, you can call 311 to find non-emergency government services. For example, you can call 311 to ask a question about garbage collection or request that your sidewalk be repaired. Some places do not offer 311 services. Call your city or town government to see if 311 is available in your area.

What to Expect When You Rent a Home

This section outlines the different steps you may encounter before moving into your new home. For more information, visit **www.hud.gov** or, for Spanish, see **www.espanol.hud.gov**.

Applying to Rent: People who rent housing are called tenants. As a tenant, you either rent housing directly from the landlord (the owner of the property) or through the property manager (a person responsible for the property). A landlord or property manager may ask you to fill out a rental application, which verifies whether you have money to pay rent.

The application may ask for your Social Security number and proof that you are working. You can use your Permanent Resident Card if you do not yet have a Social Security number, or you can show a pay stub from your job to prove you are working. You may also be asked to pay a small application fee.

If you are not yet working, you may need someone to sign the rental agreement with you. This person is called a co-signer. If you cannot pay the rent, the co-signer is responsible for paying it.

Signing a Lease: You sign a rental agreement, or lease, if the landlord agrees to rent to you. A lease is a legal document. When you sign a lease, you agree to pay your rent on time and rent for a specific length of time. Most leases are for one year. You can also find housing for shorter periods of time, such as one month. You may have to pay more money for a short lease.

When you sign a lease, you agree to keep the home clean and in good condition. You may be charged extra if you damage the place you are renting. The lease may also list the number of people who may live in the home.

Paying a Security Deposit: Renters usually pay a security deposit before moving into the home. This deposit is usually equal to one month's rent. If the home is clean and in good condition when you move out, then you will get your deposit back. If not, the landlord may keep some or all of your deposit to pay for cleaning or repairs.

Inspect the house or apartment **before** you move in. Tell the landlord about any problems you find. **Before** you move out, ask your landlord what you need to fix or clean so you may receive all of your security deposit back.

Paying Other Rental Costs: For some houses or apartments, the rent payment includes the cost of utilities, such as gas, electricity, heat, water, and trash removal. For other rentals, you must pay separately for these expenses. When you are looking for housing, ask the landlord if any utilities are included. If utilities are included, make sure this information is in your lease before you sign it. If utilities are not included, find out how much they will cost before signing the agreement. The cost of some utilities will be more in the summer (for air conditioning) or in the winter (for heat). Renters insurance, sometimes referred to as tenants insurance, is available. This insurance protects personal belongings, offers liability protection, and may cover additional living expenses if the home you are renting is destroyed or damaged.

Ending a Lease: Ending a rental agreement is called "terminating your lease." If you need to terminate your lease earlier than expected, you may have to pay monthly rent until the end of the lease even if you are not living there. You also may lose your security deposit if you leave before the end of the lease. Before you move out, give your landlord a written notice telling him or her that you are ready to move out. Most landlords require at least 30 days' advance notice before you want to leave. Before you sign the lease, make sure you understand its terms and ask how much notice you are required to give the landlord before moving out.

Addressing Home Repairs with Your Landlord

Landlords must keep the home or apartment you rent in safe and good condition. If you are in need of a home repair:

- First, talk to your landlord. Tell him or her about the problem and that you need it fixed. If your landlord does not respond, then write a letter to your landlord to tell him or her about the problem. Keep a copy of the letter for yourself.

- If your landlord still does not respond to your request, then call your local Housing Office. Most city or local governments have people who inspect homes for problems. Ask the Housing Office to send an inspector to visit your home. Show the inspector the problem.

- Lastly, if your landlord does not fix the problem(s), then you may be able to file a legal charge against your landlord.

TIP

If you move, you should tell the U.S. Postal Service so it can forward your mail to your new address. To change your address online, visit **www.usps.com/umove** or visit your local post office. Also, do not forget to file Form AR-11, Change of Address, with USCIS. See page 19 for instructions.

Know Your Rights: Discrimination in Housing Is Not Allowed

Landlords cannot refuse to rent to you because of who you are. It is against the law for landlords to reject you because of:

- Your race or color;
- Your national origin;
- Your religion;
- Your sex;
- A disability; or
- Your family status.

If you feel you have been refused housing for any of these reasons, contact the U.S. Department of Housing and Urban Development (HUD) by phone at 1-800-669-9777 or 1-800-927-9275 (for hearing impaired). You can also file a complaint in the "Fair Housing" section of **www.hud.gov**. Information is available in several languages.

Buying a Home

For many people, owning a home is part of the American dream. Owning a home has many benefits but also many responsibilities.

Real estate agents can help you find a home to buy. Ask friends or co-workers if they can recommend a real estate agent, or call a local real estate agency for the name of an agent. Ask for an agent who is familiar with the area where you want to buy a home. There are many ways to search for real estate, such as researching on the Internet, looking at real estate in the newspaper "Classifieds" section, or looking for "For Sale" signs in the neighborhoods you like.

Most people need to get a loan to pay for a home. This is called a mortgage. You can get a mortgage from a local bank or from a mortgage company. A mortgage means you are borrowing money at a specific interest rate for a specific period of time.

The interest you pay on your mortgage can be deducted from your federal income tax.

You need to buy homeowner's insurance to help pay for any possible future damage to your home. Insurance usually covers damage due to bad weather, fire, or robbery. You will also need to pay property taxes on the value of your home.

A real estate agent or real estate lawyer can help you find a mortgage and insurance. He or she can help you fill out the forms to buy your home. A real estate agent should not charge you a fee to buy a home, but you may have to pay a fee to a real estate lawyer to help you fill out the forms. You will also have to pay fees to get your mortgage and to file legal forms with the state. These fees are called closing costs. Your real estate agent or mortgage lender must tell you how much these fees will be before you sign the final purchase forms for your home. For help on looking for a real estate agent, finding a loan, and choosing insurance, visit the "Buying a Home" section of **www.hud.gov**.

TIP

Protect yourself from loan fraud and lenders who charge very high interest rates on mortgages. Some lenders may try to take advantage of you, such as by charging you more money because you are new to this country. There are laws to protect you from fraud, unnecessary expenses, and discrimination in buying a home. For more information about loan fraud and advice on preventing it, visit the "Buying a Home" section of **www.hud.gov**.

Look for a Job

There are many ways to look for a job in the United States. To increase your chances of finding a job, you can:

- Ask friends, neighbors, family members, or other people in your community about job openings or good places to work.

- Search for jobs on the Internet. If you use a computer at your library, ask the library staff to help you get started.

- Look for "Help Wanted" signs in the windows of local businesses.

- Go to the employment or human resources offices of businesses in your area to ask about job openings.

- Visit community agencies that help immigrants find jobs and that administer job-training programs.

- Check bulletin boards at local libraries, grocery stores, and community centers for hiring notices.

- Check with the department of employment services for your state or locality.

- Look in the newspaper's "Classifieds" section under "Employment."

While you are looking for a job, you may come across employment scams. Although many job placement firms are legitimate and helpful, others may misrepresent their services, promote outdated or fake job offerings, or charge high up-front fees for services that may not lead to a job. For more information, visit **www.ftc.gov/jobscams**.

Applying for a Job

Most employers will ask you to fill out a job application. This is a form with questions about your address, education, and past work experience. It may also ask for information about people you have worked with in the past who can recommend you. These people are called references, and the employer may want to call them to ask questions about you.

You may need to create a résumé with a list of your work experience. A résumé tells your employer about your past jobs, your education and training, and your job skills. When you apply for a job, take your résumé with you.

A good résumé:

- Has your name, address, phone number, and email address;

- Lists your past jobs and includes dates worked;

- Shows your level of education;

- Shows any special skills you have; and

- Is easy to read and has no mistakes.

Check with local community service agencies to see if they can help you write a résumé. Private businesses can help with this too, but they may charge a fee. For more information about applying for a job, visit **www.careeronestop.org**.

What Are Benefits?

In addition to your pay, some employers provide extra employment benefits. Benefits may include:

- Medical care

- Dental care

- Eye care

- Life insurance

- A retirement plan

Employers may pay some or all of the costs of these benefits. If you are offered a job, ask which benefits the employer provides to employees.

The Job Interview

Employers may want to meet with you to talk about the job. They will ask about your past work and your skills. To help prepare for the interview, you can practice answering questions about your past work and your skills with a friend or family member. You can also ask questions to the employer at the end of the interview. This is a good chance to learn more about the job.

You may want to ask:

- How would you describe a typical day in this position?

- How would I be trained or introduced to the job?

- Where does the job fit into the organization?

- How would you describe the work environment?

- What do you consider the positive aspects and challenging aspects of this position?

During the interview, an employer can ask you many questions, but employers are not allowed to ask certain questions. No one should ask you questions about your race, color, sex, family status, religion, national origin, age, or any disability you may have. For more information about the job interview process, visit **www.dol.gov**.

Know Your Rights: Federal Laws Protect Employees

The United States has several federal laws that forbid employers from discriminating against people looking for a job and that protect against retaliation and other forms of discrimination in the workplace.

- The Civil Rights Act forbids discrimination on the basis of race, color, religion, country of origin, sex, or pregnancy.

- The Age Discrimination in Employment Act forbids discrimination on the basis of age.

- The Americans with Disabilities Act and the Rehabilitation Act forbids discrimination on the basis of having a disability.

- The Equal Pay Act forbids discrimination on the basis of sex.

- The Genetic Nondiscrimination Act forbids discrimination on the basis of genetic information.

For more information about these protections, visit the U.S. Equal Employment Opportunity Commission website at **www.eeoc.gov** or call 1-800-669-4000 and 1-800-669-6820 (for hearing impaired).

Other laws help keep workplaces safe, provide leave in cases of family or medical emergencies, and provide temporary funds for unemployed workers. Visit the U.S. Department of Labor website at **www.dol.gov** for more information about workers' rights.

Additionally, federal laws protect employees from discrimination on the basis of national origin or citizenship status. For more information about these protections, call the Department of Justice's Office of Special Counsel for Immigration-Related Unfair Employment Practices at 1-800-255-7688 or 1-800-237-2515 (for hearing impaired). If you do not speak English, interpreters are available to help you. For more information, visit **www.justice.gov/crt/osc**.

What to Expect When You Are Hired

When you go to your new job for the first time, you will be asked to fill out some forms. These include:

- **Form I-9, Employment Eligibility Verification:** By law, employers must verify that all newly hired workers are eligible to work in the United States. On your first day of work, you will need to fill out Section 1 of Form I-9. You should not be asked to fill out Section 1 until you have accepted a job. Within three business days, you must give your employer documentation that shows your identity and authorization to work. You can choose which document(s) to show as proof of your right to work in the United States, as long as the document is listed on Form I-9. Your employer will provide you with the list of acceptable documents. Examples of acceptable documents are your Permanent Resident Card or an unrestricted Social Security card in combination with a state-issued driver's license. For more information, visit I-9 Central at **www.uscis.gov/I-9Central**.

- **Form W-4, Employee's Withholding Allowance Certificate:** Your employer should take federal taxes from your paycheck to send to the government. This is called withholding tax. Form W-4 tells your employer to withhold taxes and helps you determine the correct amount to withhold so that your tax bill is not due all at once at the end of the year.

- **Other Forms:** You may need to fill out a tax withholding form for the state you live in and other forms so that you can get benefits.

You may be paid each week, every two weeks, or once a month. Your paycheck will show the amount taken out for federal and state taxes, Social Security taxes, and any employment benefits you pay. Some employers will send your pay directly to your bank account; this method is called direct deposit.

Confirming Your Eligibility to Work

E-Verify is an Internet-based system that employers use to compare information from an employee's Form I-9, Employment Eligibility Verification, to USCIS and Social Security Administration (SSA) records to confirm that an employee is authorized to work in the United States. Some employers must participate in E-Verify; other employers participate voluntarily. To learn more about E-Verify, visit **www.uscis.gov/e-verify**.

To Confirm Your Eligibility on Your Own

Self Check is a free, Internet-based application that you can use to check your employment eligibility if you are in the United States and over the age of 16. After you enter the required information, Self Check will compare that information with various government databases to determine your work eligibility in the United States. For more information, visit **www.uscis.gov/selfcheck** or, for Spanish, **www.uscis.gov/selfcheck/Espanol**.

Speaking English at Work

If you do not speak English, try to learn it as soon as possible. You can find free or low-cost English language classes in your community, often through the local public schools or community college. Knowing English will help you in your job, your community, and your daily life. See page 68 for more information about learning English.

If your employer says you **must** speak English at work, then he or she must show that speaking English is required for you to do your job correctly. Your employer must also tell you that English is required **before** you are hired. If your employer cannot show that speaking English is required for your job, then he or she may be breaking a federal law. If you need assistance or more information, you can contact the U.S. Equal Employment Opportunity Commission (EEOC). Call 1-800-669-4000 or 1-800-669-6820 (for hearing impaired) or visit **www.eeoc.gov**.

Drug Tests and Background Checks

For some jobs, you may be required to take a test to make sure that you are not using illegal drugs. Some jobs require a background check, which is an investigation into your past activities and present circumstances.

Federal Protection for Immigrant Workers

Many immigrants (including permanent residents) and all U.S. citizens are protected against workplace discrimination. Federal law says that employers cannot discriminate against you because of your immigration status. Employers cannot:

- Refuse to hire or fire you because of your immigration status or because you are not a U.S. citizen.

- Require you to show a Permanent Resident Card or reject your employment authorization documentation.

- Hire undocumented workers.

- Discriminate against you because of your national origin or country of origin.

- Retaliate against any employee who complains of the above treatment.

For more information about your rights or to file a complaint, call the Department of Justice's Office of Special Counsel for Immigration-Related Unfair Employment Practices at 1-800-255-7688 or 1-800-237-2515 (for hearing impaired). If you do not speak English, interpreters are available to help you. For more information, visit **www.justice.gov/crt/osc**.

Child Care

Do not leave young children at home alone. If you work and your children are too young to go to school, you need to find someone to watch them while you are at work. Sometimes school-age children need someone to watch them after school. If you or other family members are not able to watch your children after school, you need to find someone to take care of them. Otherwise, there may be serious legal consequences. For more information on laws and guidelines in your state, contact your local child protective services agency.

Finding Child Care

Choosing someone to care for your children is an important decision. As you make this decision, think about the quality and cost of care. Try to find a caregiver who is close to your home or job.

There are many resources you can use to find a good child care provider. Ask other parents, friends, and co-workers who they have caring for their children. Some states have a child care referral agency that can give you a list of state-licensed child care programs. Licensed child care programs meet specific requirements set by the state for the protection of your children. You also can call your local school district office to find places where other children in your neighborhood receive care.

TIP

If you need help finding good child care in your area, visit **www.usa.gov/Topics/Parents-Care.shtml**.

Types of Child Care

You have a number of choices when choosing a child care provider, such as:

- A caregiver comes into your home to watch your children. This type of service can be expensive because your child gets more individual attention. The quality of care depends on the person you hire.

- Your child is cared for in somebody else's home with a small group of other children. This option can be less expensive than other types of child care. The quality of care depends on the people who watch your child and the number of children they are caring for in their home.

- Child care centers located in schools, churches, faith-based organizations, and other places. These programs usually have several caregivers who watch larger groups of children. Child care centers must meet state standards, and the staff is usually required to have special training and experience.

- Head Start Programs, called "Early Head Start" and "Head Start," are programs funded by the federal government for low-income families. These programs provide care and educational services to young children to get them ready for school. To learn more about these programs, call the U.S. Department of Health and Human Services at 1-866-763-6481 or visit **http://eclkc.ohs.acf.hhs.gov/hslc**.

Some child care providers will take care of children for a full day or only part of the day, depending on the parents' needs. Cost is also a factor in choosing a caregiver. Check to see if you are eligible for federal or state child care assistance. Many states offer financial assistance to low-income parents who are working or participating in job-training or education programs. For more information about federal or state child care assistance, visit the "Education and Child Care" section of **www.welcometousa.gov**.

How Can You Tell If a Child Care Provider Is Good?

Think about these basic questions when you visit a child care program:

- Are the children happy when around the staff?

- Are toys that are appropriate for the children's ages available?

- Are children doing an appropriate activity?

- Does the provider talk to your child while you are there?

- Is the space clean and organized?

- What is the curriculum or routine for the children?

Ask for references so that you can talk to other parents about the program.

Transportation

There are many ways to travel in the United States. Many cities have different forms of public transportation, such as buses, trains, or streetcars. Anyone can ride public transportation for a small fee. In some places, you can buy a card to use for several trips on trains or buses. You can also pay for each trip separately. Taxicabs, or taxis, are cars with drivers who take you where you want to go for a fee. Taxis are more expensive than public transportation.

Getting a Driver's License

It is against the law to drive without a driver's license. You must apply for and get a driver's license if you want to drive. You get your driver's license in the state where you live.

Check with the state office that issues driver's licenses to find out how to get one. These offices have different names in each state. Some common names are Department of Motor Vehicles, Department of Transportation, Motor Vehicle Administration, or Department of Public Safety. You can find these offices in the phone book or for more information, visit **www.usa.gov/ Topics/Motor_Vehicles.shtml**.

Some permanent residents already have a driver's license from another country. You may be able to trade it for a driver's license in your state. Check with your state office to see if you can.

Should I Buy a Car?

Owning a car can be a convenient way to travel. In the United States, you must also pay for car insurance and register your vehicle and license plates. Heavy traffic can make driving difficult in some cities. Think of all the costs and benefits before you decide to buy a car. For more information on buying a car, visit the "Travel and Recreation" section of **www.usa.gov**.

10 Tips for Driving Safely in the United States

1. Drive on the right-hand side of the road.

2. Always have your driver's license, registration, and insurance card with you.

3. Always wear your seat belt.

4. Use proper seat belts and car safety seats for children.

5. Use your car's signals to show if you are turning left or right.

6. Obey all traffic laws and signals.

7. Pull over to the side of the road if an emergency vehicle—such as police car, fire truck, or ambulance—needs to pass you.

8. Do not pass a school bus when its red lights are flashing.

9. Do not drive if you have been drinking or taking drugs.

10. Slow down and be very careful when driving in fog, ice, rain, or snow.

A driver's license is used for identification in the United States. It is a good idea to get one even if you do not own or regularly drive a car.

If you do not know how to drive, you can take driving lessons. Many public school districts have classes in driver education. You can also look under "Driving Instruction" in the yellow pages of the phone book.

TIP

Hitchhiking is not common in the United States. In many places, it is illegal. For safety reasons, do not hitchhike and do not give rides to hitchhikers.

Taking Care of Your Money

Taking care of your money can have a big impact on your future in the United States. This section discusses personal finances, paying taxes, and ways in which you can protect yourself and your money.

Personal Finance

Getting an Account

In the United States, two types of financial institutions that offer personal financing accounts are banks and credit unions.

A bank account is a safe place to keep your money. Banks have different kinds of accounts. Checking accounts and savings accounts are two common ones. You can open an account for yourself or a joint account with your spouse or another person. Banks may charge you fees for some of their services.

A credit union is another place to safeguard your money. Your employer may have a credit union that you can join, or you may be able to join one, depending on where you live. Credit unions provide most of the same services as banks but may offer extra services. Compare the services, fees, coverage, hours, and locations of financial institutions before you open an account so you can choose one that best meets your needs.

When you open an account, you will be asked to prove your identity. You can use your Permanent Resident Card or driver's license. You will also need to give the financial institution some money—called a deposit—to put into your new account. When you take money out of your account, this transaction is called a withdrawal. You can withdraw money by writing a check, going to an automated teller machine (ATM), or filling out a withdrawal form at your financial institution.

TIP

There are stores that offer check-cashing services and overseas money-wiring services, which cost extra. Check to see if your bank or credit union offers these services at a lower cost.

Keeping Your Money Safe

It is not safe to carry around large amounts of cash or to leave cash in your home, it could be stolen or lost. If you put money in a bank or credit union that is a member of the Federal Deposit Insurance Corporation (FDIC) or is insured by the National Credit Union Administration (NCUA), then your money is protected up to $250,000. When choosing a financial institution, make sure it is either a member of the FDIC or that it is insured by the NCUA. For more information, visit **www.fdic.gov** or **www.ncua.gov**.

Using Your Account

You can get money from your account by using a personal check, ATM, or debit card. Be sure that only you and your joint account holder (if you have one) have access to your account.

Personal Checks: You can get a supply of personal checks when you open your checking account. These checks are forms that you fill out to pay for something. Checks tell your financial institution to pay the person or business you have written on the check. Keep these checks in a safe place and ask your financial institution how to order new checks when you have used your supply.

ATM Cards: You can ask your financial institution for an ATM card. An ATM card is a small plastic card linked to your account. Use this card to get cash or deposit money in your account at an ATM. Usually you do not pay a fee for using your own financial institution's ATM. You will most likely be charged a fee if you use an ATM owned and operated by another financial institution.

The financial institution staff will show you how to use an ATM card and give you a special number, called a PIN (personal identification number), to use at the ATM. Be careful when using ATMs. Never give anyone your PIN or ATM card because he or she could use it to take money out of your account.

Debit Cards: Your financial institution may give you a debit card to use for your checking account. Sometimes your ATM card can also be used as a debit card. Never give anyone your PIN or debit card because he or she could use it to take money out of your account. You can use your debit card to pay for something at a store and the money will automatically be taken out of your checking account to pay the store.

Cashier's and Certified Checks: These are checks that a financial institution creates upon your request. You give the financial institution money and then they create a check for that amount of money to the person or business you want to pay. Financial institutions may charge a fee for these checks. Ask your financial institution about other options that may be available to you.

TIP

Manage your account carefully so that you do not incur any overdraft fees. An overdraft occurs when you do not have enough money in your account to cover a payment or withdrawal. Check with your financial institution to find out about your options and the fees.

Credit Cards

Credit cards allow you to make purchases and pay for them later. Banks, credit unions, stores, and gas stations are some businesses that can give you a credit card. You get a bill in the mail each month for purchases you have made with your credit card. If you pay the entire amount on the bill when you receive it, then you do not have to pay interest. If you do not pay the entire amount or if you send your payment late, then you will be charged interest and possibly an additional fee. Some credit cards have very high interest rates, so review the different credit card options to determine which one is best for you. Credit cards may be called charge cards, but they are different. With a charge card you are required to pay the balance in full each month, but credit cards allow you to carry a balance if you do not pay in full.

Be careful about giving your credit card number to others, especially over the phone or on the Internet. Be sure you know and trust the person or business that asks for your number.

TIP

Check your credit card bill each month to make sure all the charges are correct. If you see a charge that you did not make, call the credit card company immediately. You usually do not have to pay for charges you did not make if you report it to the credit card company immediately.

Write down the numbers for all accounts and debit, ATM, and credit cards. Also write down the phone numbers of these companies. Keep this information in a safe and secure place. If your wallet is lost or stolen, call the companies and cancel all of your cards. This will keep someone else from using your cards illegally.

To learn more about personal finance, visit **www.mymoney.gov**.

Your Credit Rating

In the United States, the way you manage your credit is very important. There are organizations that determine your credit score or credit rating. Your credit score or rating depends on how you pay bills, how many loans you take out, how many credit cards you have, and other factors. Your credit rating is very important when you want to buy a home or car, or take out a loan. Here are things you can do to maintain a good credit rating:

- Pay all your bills on time.

- Keep your credit card balances low and pay at least the minimum amount due each month.

Under federal law, you can get one free credit report once a year. If you would like to get a copy of your credit rating report, call 1-877-322-8228 or visit **www.annualcreditreport.com**.

Paying Taxes

Taxes are money paid by people to federal, state, and local governments. Taxes pay for services provided by the government. There are different types of taxes, such as income tax, sales tax, and property tax.

Income Tax: Income tax is paid to federal, most state, and some local governments. Taxable income is money that you get from wages, self-employment, tips, and the sale of property. Most people pay income taxes by having money withheld from their paychecks. The amount of income tax you must pay depends on how much money you earn. Income tax rates are lower for people who make less money. Anyone who earns income, resides in the United States, and meets certain requirements needs to file a tax return and pay all taxes owed.

The Internal Revenue Service (IRS) is the federal agency that collects income tax. Taxpayers file Form 1040, U.S. Individual Income Tax Return, with the IRS each year. Your tax return tells the government how much you earned and how much in taxes was taken out of your paycheck. If you had too much taken out of your paycheck in taxes, you will receive a refund. If you did not have enough taken out of your paycheck in taxes, you will be required to pay the IRS.

Social Security and Medicare Taxes: These federal taxes are withheld from your paycheck. Social Security provides benefits for certain retired workers and their families, certain disabled workers and their families, and certain family members of deceased workers. Medicare taxes pay for medical services for most people over age 65. In most cases, you must work a total of 10 years (or 40 quarters) over the course of your life to receive Social Security retirement benefits and Medicare benefits. You may need fewer than 10 years of work to receive disability benefits or for your family to get survivors' benefits based on your earnings.

Sales Taxes: Sales taxes are state and local taxes. These taxes are added to the cost of buying certain things. Sales taxes are based on the cost of the item. Revenue collected from sales taxes helps pay for state and local government services, such as roads, police, and fire departments.

Property Taxes: Property taxes are state and local taxes on your house and/or land. In most places, property taxes help support local public schools and other services.

Your W-2 Form: Wage and Tax Statement

A W-2 is a federal form that lists your earnings and the taxes you paid for the last tax year. A tax year is from January 1 to December 31. By law, your employer must send you a W-2 form by January 31 each year. You will receive a W-2 form for each job you have. You must send a copy of your W-2 form with your federal income tax return to the IRS. If you live or work in a state that collects income tax, then you must send a copy of your W-2 with your state income tax return.

Getting Help with Your Taxes

As a permanent resident, you are required to file a federal income tax return every year. This return covers your earnings from January to December of the past year. You must file your return by April 15. You can get free help with your tax return at an IRS Taxpayer Assistance Center.

Taxpayer Assistance Centers are located in communities across the United States. To find a Taxpayer Assistance Center where you live, visit **www.irs.gov/localcontacts/index.html**. To get help by phone, call the IRS at 1-800-829-1040 or 1-800-829-4059 (for hearing impaired). For a list of current tax credits, visit **www.benefits.gov**.

How Government Works for Us

Taxes pay for the services the federal government provides to the people of the United States. Examples of these services are:

- Keeping our country safe and secure;

- Curing and preventing diseases through research;

- Educating children and adults;

- Building and maintaining our roads and highways;

- Providing medical services for low-income residents and the elderly; and

- Giving emergency help when natural disasters, such as hurricanes, floods, or earthquakes strike.

Protect Yourself and Your Money

Avoid Identity Theft

Identity theft means someone has stolen your personal information, such as your Social Security or bank account numbers. They can use it to take money from your accounts or open a credit card in your name. Identity theft is a serious crime. Protect yourself by:

- Making sure you know and trust the people or businesses you give your personal information to, especially on the phone or the Internet.

- Leaving your Social Security card at home in a safe place. Do not carry it with you.

- Carrying with you only the identification documents or credit cards you need at the time. Leave the rest at home in a safe place.

- Tearing up or shredding any paper or forms with your personal information on them before throwing them in the trash.

- Selecting unique passwords for each account. Do not use the same password, as that could put your personal information at risk.

To protect yourself against identity theft, call the Federal Trade Commission's ID Theft Hotline at 1-877-438-4338 or visit **www.consumer.ftc.gov/ features/feature-0014-identity-theft**.

"Phishing" and Other Scams

According to the Federal Trade Commission (FTC), "phishing" is when an unknown source sends an email or pop-up message to you claiming to be from a business or organization with which you are associated, such as a bank, an online payment service, or even a government agency. The message may include links to websites asking you to update your account or personal information. The links in the email connect to a website that looks like a legitimate organization's site, but the website is not real. Scammers created the website to steal your identity so that they can charge money or commit crimes in your name.

Be aware of phone scams that target individuals, including immigrants. A scammer may call you and ask for money or threaten you. They will likely have some information about you and their phone number may look like an official one. Government agencies will never call you to ask for money or threaten you. If you receive a call like this, hang up and call the official number for the business or government agency to check if it is a scam.

To avoid getting scammed, here are important things to remember:

- If you get an email or pop-up message that asks for personal or financial information, do not reply.

- Do not give out your account number or password over the phone unless you're making the call to a company you know is reputable. If you have questions about a company, check with your local consumer protection office or Better Business Bureau.

- Review credit card and bank account statements as soon as you receive them to check for unauthorized charges.

- If you have a computer, use anti-virus and anti-spyware software, as well as a firewall. Update them regularly.

- Be careful when opening attachments or downloading files from emails. If you do not know who sent the message to you, do not open the attachment(s) or download the file(s).

- If you suspect an email or website is fraudulent, report this information to the real bank, company, or government agency.

If you believe you have been scammed, you can file a complaint through the FTC's website at **www.ftccomplaintassistant.gov**. To learn more about how to avoid online scams and deal with deceptive spam, visit **www.onguardonline. gov**.

Understanding Education and Health Care

Education can help connect you and your family to your community. This section describes schools in the United States for children, youths, and adults. This section also discusses the health care system and provides resources so that you and your family can stay informed.

Education in the United States

To make sure all children are prepared to succeed, the United States provides free public education from kindergarten through grade 12 for all students in the United States. Some communities also offer the chance for children as young as three years old to attend preschool. This section tells you how to enroll your children in school, how schools in the United States work, and how to help your children learn.

Most public schools in the United States are coeducational. Coeducational means that girls and boys attend classes together, however, there are some schools that only enroll a single gender. Most schools are part of a school district that has several schools, including different schools for children of different ages. The ages of students at each school may vary from community to community.

Enroll Your Child in School

One of the first things you should do is to enroll your child in school. Call or visit your local school district's main office or website to find out which school or schools your child may attend. Currently, all states and the District of Columbia have compulsory school attendance laws. Compulsory school attendance means that all children who are between certain ages must attend school. In most states, these laws cover all children ages 5 to 16. Check with your local school district or state department of education to find out the required ages for school attendance in your state.

You can send your child to a public or private school. Public schools are free and do not offer religious instruction. The state decides what your child learns in public school, but local school districts, principals, teachers, and parents decide how to teach your child. Charter schools are a special type of public school that operate independently from the local school district. Your local and state taxes, and some of your federal taxes, pay for public schools.

Private schools are another way you can educate your child. Private schools are owned and run by groups that are independent of the government, including religious and non-religious groups. Students generally must pay a fee (called tuition) to attend private school. In some cases, private schools may offer financial help for students who cannot pay the tuition. In other cases, public funds may be available in the form of vouchers for students to attend private school. Some private schools are coeducational, while some are only for boys or only for girls. Some states have licensing or registration requirements for private schools, and many private schools choose to be accredited by an accrediting association. To learn more about private schools, contact your state's department of education.

Educating your child at home is another option. This is called homeschooling. The requirements for homeschooling differ from state to state. Parents interested in homeschooling should contact their state department of education to get more information.

Most American children are in public school for around 13 years, from kindergarten through grade 12. In most schools, your child will be placed in a class (called a grade) based on two things: age and level of previous education. In some cases, a school may give your child a test to determine his or her grade level and class assignment.

HOW THE TYPICAL U.S. SCHOOL IS ORGANIZED		
School	Grades	Ages
Elementary or Primary School	Kindergarten and Grades 1 to 5 or 1 to 6	Children Ages 5 to 11
Junior or Middle School	Grades 6 to 8, 7 to 8, or 7 to 9	Youths Ages 11 to 14
Secondary or High School	Grades 9 to 12 or 10 to 12	Young Adults Ages 14 to 18 (and up to age 21 in some cases)
Postsecondary or Higher Education	Public and Private Community Colleges, Two-Year or Four-Year Colleges or Universities, Trade Schools	All Eligible Adults May Attend

Here is a list of answers to questions that parents often ask about public schools:

How long is the school year?

The school year usually begins in August or September and ends in May or June. In some places, children attend school all year. Children are in school Monday through Friday. Many schools offer programs before or after regular school hours for children whose parents work. You may be charged a fee for these before- or after-school programs, but some special tutoring services may be available for free in your school district.

Where do I enroll my child?

Call or visit your local school district's main office or website to find out which school or schools your child may attend.

What documents do I need to enroll my child?

You need your child's medical records and proof that your child has certain immunizations (also called shots) to protect him or her from disease. You also may need proof of identification, such as a birth certificate, and proof that you live in the same community as the school. If you have lost these documents, ask school staff how to get new documents. To avoid delays, do this before you try to enroll your child.

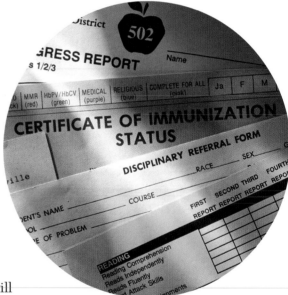

What if my child does not speak English?

If your child does not speak English, the school district will evaluate your child's language skills. The school will then provide your child with the services he or she needs to learn English and to participate in the academic program for his or her grade level. The school district is responsible for providing your child with the right services to meet your child's language needs, and for informing you in a language you can understand about the services your child will receive. You can contact your child's school to ask about this process. In addition to language services during the regular school day, some schools offer after-school programs and tutoring to help students improve English outside of school. Your child's school will tell you what kind of extra help they offer to students learning English.

What if my child has a disability?

All students in the United States have the right to get a free public education, whether or not they have a disability. If your child has a disability, he or she may receive free special education and related services. Your child will be placed in a regular school classroom if appropriate for his or her needs. Sometimes your child may need special education or related services outside the regular classroom. You can participate when school staff make individualized decisions about how to best teach your child. The school is responsible for communicating with you about these decisions in a language that you can understand. For more information on how to access services and other resources, visit **http://idea.ed.gov**.

My child was not in school before coming to the United States. How long can he or she attend public school for free?

In most states, students can attend public school for free until they graduate high school or reach the maximum age, which is usually age 21. If a student is under age 22, they may be able to enroll in a high school and pursue a regular high school diploma. If a student has not graduated from high school by age 22, he or she can enroll in Adult Secondary Education (ASE) classes. ASE classes help prepare students to obtain the recognized equivalent of a high school diploma (such as a General Educational Development [GED] certificate) instead of a regular high school diploma. Call your local school district office or state department of education, or research online, to find out where GED or other high school equivalency classes are offered.

How will my child get to school?

Children can sometimes walk to school in the United States. If the school is too far away or if it is not safe to walk, they may ride a school bus or take public transportation, such as a subway or train. Many public schools have free buses that pick up and drop off students at a school bus stop near your home. Other public schools provide eligible students with passes so that they can ride local public transportation for free or at a reduced cost. To find out if your child can ride a bus to school or receive a public transportation pass, contact your local school district office. If you have a car, you can also set up a car pool with other parents in your area to share driving your children to school.

Federal School Meals Program

To improve learning, the U.S. government provides healthy low-cost or free meals to more than 26 million children each school day. Participation in the School Breakfast Program and National School Lunch Program is based on family income and size. The Special Milk Program provides milk to children who do not participate in other federal school meals programs. For more information about these U.S. Department of Agriculture programs, visit **www.fns. usda.gov/cnd**.

What will my child eat at school?

Children can take lunch to school or buy it at the school cafeteria. The U.S. government also provides nutritious free or low-cost breakfast and lunch for eligible children who cannot afford to buy food at school. Call or visit your child's school to find out if it participates in the federal school meals program. Talk with school staff to find out if your children are eligible to participate.

Who pays for books and school activities?

Public schools usually provide free books. Students must usually buy their own school supplies, such as paper and pencils. If you cannot pay for these supplies, contact your child's school. Some schools may charge a small fee for supplies or special events, such as school trips. Many schools offer after-school sports and music programs. You may need to pay a fee for your child to participate in some of these programs.

What will my child learn?

Each state sets academic standards for schools. These standards outline what all students should know and at what level they are expected to perform. Local school districts decide how this information should be taught. Most schools teach English, math, social studies, science, and physical education. Art, music, and foreign languages are sometimes offered, too.

How is my child's work assessed?

Teachers assign scores (also called grades) based on the work children do during the school year. Grades are usually based on homework, classwork, tests, attendance, and class behavior. Your child will receive a report card several times a year. Some schools will send your child's report card directly to you. A report card tells you how your child is doing in each subject. Schools have different ways of grading students. Some schools use letter grades, with A or A+ for excellent work and D or F for poor or failing work. Others use number grades or words like "excellent," "good," or "needs improvement" to summarize your child's performance. In many grades, students also take standardized tests, which schools administer to assess students. Ask school staff how students in your child's school are graded and assessed.

How can I talk to my child's teacher?

Most schools have regular parent conferences for you to meet with your child's teacher. You can also schedule meetings to talk with teachers or school administrators about how your child is doing in school. If you do not speak or understand English, the school district will provide a qualified interpreter for such meetings. The school district is also required to provide you with information on other school matters in a language you understand.

What if my child misses school?

Being in school is very important. Parents must send a written letter to the teacher or call the school to explain why their child was not in school. If your child will be out of school, tell the teacher in advance. Students must usually make up any work they missed. Ask your child's school what type of information you need to provide if your child misses school.

What if my child gets into trouble?

Many schools have a list of rules or a discipline policy that students must obey, often called a code of conduct. Ask your child's school about its discipline policy or code of conduct. The school may discipline students who break school rules by requiring them to stay after the school day is over or by banning them from participating in sports or other school activities. Physical punishment is not permitted in U.S. schools in most states.

Children may be suspended or expelled from school if they behave very badly and break school rules often. If your child is expelled, he or she will no longer be able to go to the same school. You will need to meet with school staff to find out how to get your child back into a school.

Is my child safe in school?

Most American public schools are safe places to learn. If you are worried about your child's safety, talk to a teacher, school counselor, principal, or other administrator.

How to Stop Bullying

Bullying is unwanted, aggressive verbal or physical behavior among school-aged children. Bullying can occur during or after school hours. While most reported bullying happens in the school building, bullying also happens in places like the playground, bus, or on the Internet. To learn more about how to prevent bullying or respond to it, visit **www.stopbullying.gov**.

Higher Education: Colleges and Universities

After high school, young adults and other adults can continue their education in a two-year community or technical college, a four-year college, or a university. These are called postsecondary institutions or institutions of higher education. Typically, the first four years of postsecondary education is called undergraduate education, and schooling beyond the bachelor's degree is called graduate studies. There are both public and private institutions of higher education. Generally, public colleges and universities may cost less than private ones, especially for residents of the state where the college or university is located. Adults can also choose to attend schools to learn how to do specific jobs, such as repairing computers or being a health care assistant.

Students in higher education choose a specific subject to study in depth (this subject is called their major). Choosing a major helps prepare them for employment or further education in that field.

HIGHER EDUCATION		
Degree Type	Type of School	Years of Schooling
Certificate	Community College/Trade School	Six Months to Two Years
Associate's	Community College	Two Years
Bachelor's	Four-Year College or University	Four Years
Master's	University	Two Years
Doctorate	University	Two to Eight Years
Professional	Specialized School	Two to Five Years

A college or university education can be expensive, but there are programs to help you pay for the cost of education. Most students take out a loan or apply for scholarships or financial aid to help pay for their schooling. Some schools provide financial support called scholarships. You can visit your school's financial aid office to learn more about scholarships. Certain scholarships and grants are limited to U.S. citizens, U.S. nationals, permanent residents, or other eligible non-U.S. citizens. The U.S. government also provides financial aid for students. To learn more about financial aid, see below or visit **www.StudentAid.gov**.

Federal Financial Aid for College Students

The U.S. government provides financial aid to help students pay for their education expenses at an eligible college, technical school, vocational school, or graduate school. Federal financial aid covers expenses such as tuition, fees, room and board, book supplies, and transportation. Students generally qualify for this aid based on their financial need, not their grades. There are three types of federal aid:

- Grants: money that you do not have to repay.

- Work study: money that you earn by working while you are in school.

- Loans: money that you borrow now but must repay later with interest.

For more information on federal financial aid programs, call 1-800-433-3243 or visit the U.S. Department of Education website at **www.StudentAid.ed.gov/resources**. Information is also available in Spanish.

Beware of Financial Aid Fraud

Be careful when you are searching for information about student financial assistance. Avoid offers that seem too good to be true or that promise you results in exchange for money. Every year, families lose millions of dollars to scholarship fraud. If you are the victim of fraud or for more information, call the Federal Trade Commission at 1-877-382-4357 or 1-866-653-4261 (for hearing impaired). You can also visit their website at **www.consumer.ftc.gov/articles/0082-scholarship-and-financial-aid-scams**.

Adult Education

Learning does not have to end when you become an adult. In the United States, people are encouraged to become lifelong learners. If you are 16 years of age or older and have not completed high school, you can enroll in Adult Secondary Education (ASE) classes. These classes prepare you to earn the recognized equivalent of a high school diploma (such as a General Educational Development [GED] certificate).

A GED certificate is the most well-known equivalent to a high school diploma, although some states may require that you take another test that is similar to the GED or meet other requirements in order to obtain a high school equivalency diploma or certificate. A high school equivalency diploma or certificate (such as a GED) shows that you have learned high school-level academic knowledge and skills. To earn a GED, you must pass tests in four different areas: reasoning through language arts (reading and writing), social studies, science, and mathematical reasoning. Most U.S. employers consider a GED credential to be equal to a regular high school diploma. In many areas, GED preparation classes are free or low cost. Search the Internet for GED and other adult education courses, or call your local school district office for information.

Many adults take classes to learn more about a subject that interests them or to learn new skills that can help them in their jobs. Many public school systems and local community colleges offer a wide range of adult education classes. Typically, these classes have low fees and anyone can enroll. Check with your local school system or community college to find out what classes are available, how much they cost, and how you can enroll.

Learn English

There are many places where you can learn how to speak, read, and write in English. Many children and adults enroll in English as a second language (ESL) classes. ESL classes help people who do not know English learn the language. These classes are also called English for Speakers of Other Languages (ESOL) or English literacy classes.

Children who do not know English will learn it in school. America's public schools provide help and instruction for all students who need to learn English.

Adults who do not understand English can enroll in an ESL class offered in a public adult and community education program or a private language school. Your child's school may offer family literacy services, parent outreach, and training for parents of non-English speakers. Contact your child's school to find out if it offers these programs.

School districts and community colleges often offer public adult and community education programs in local communities. These programs may provide ESL classes along with tutoring from local volunteers. These programs are often free or may charge a small fee. Classes may meet during day or evening hours. Call your local community college or school district office to learn about ESL classes they offer.

Most large cities also have private language schools that offer day or evening ESL classes. The cost for private language classes is often based on the number of hours of instruction, and they are generally more expensive than public classes. You can search the Internet for private language schools in your area.

Some community organizations, libraries, and religious groups also offer free or low-cost ESL classes. Check with your local public library, social service agency, or place of worship. The reference librarian at the local library may tell you about ESL programs and show you where to find ESL books, tapes, CDs, and computer software at the library.

To find the nearest ESL program, visit **www.literacydirectory.org**. You can also study online by visiting **www.usalearns.org**.

Health Care

Generally, people in the United States pay for their own medical care either directly or through insurance. Medical care is expensive, so it is beneficial to work for an employer that offers you health insurance or to buy health insurance on your own. It is important that you and your family get health insurance as soon as possible.

Employers may offer health insurance as a benefit to their employees. Some employers pay for all of your monthly health care coverage cost while some pay only part of the cost. This monthly cost is called a premium. You may need to pay part of the premium. Usually, employers will deduct your part of the premium from your paycheck. Some employers will also allow you to buy insurance for your family. You will probably have to pay more for this coverage.

If you have health insurance, doctors may send their bills to your health insurance company. The health insurance company may pay some or all of these bills. Often you must pay an amount to the doctor or service provider each time you use their health care services. This is sometimes called a co-payment.

If you do not have health insurance, some doctors will expect you to pay for the full cost of your care. You may be able to get federal or state health care assistance. States provide some type of assistance to low-income children, pregnant women, and people living with disabilities. Some states have additional state-funded assistance programs.

If you need immediate medical care, you can go to the emergency room of the nearest hospital to receive treatment. Most hospitals with emergency departments are required by federal law to treat individuals with an urgent medical condition even if the person cannot pay, however, the health care providers may issue a bill for the medical services provided.

When making decisions about your health, it is important to know where to get the latest, most reliable information. For a wide range of resources on health-related topics, visit **www.healthfinder.gov**.

Health Insurance Marketplace

The Health Insurance Marketplace (or health insurance exchange) is a way to find quality health insurance that fits your budget and meets your needs. It can help if you do not have affordable insurance from your employer or if you do not qualify for coverage under Medicare, Medicaid, or Children's Health Insurance Program (CHIP). The Marketplace will allow you to compare certain types of private health insurance plans, get answers to questions, find out if you are eligible for financial support to help pay for the cost of coverage, and enroll in a health care plan that meets your needs. Permanent residents and certain other people with lawful immigration status may qualify for Marketplace insurance. For the most up to date information, visit **www. HealthCare.gov**.

Finding a Low-Cost Health Care Facility

Most communities have at least one health care facility that provides free or low-cost services. These are sometimes called clinics or community health centers. To find this type of resource near you, search the Internet or ask an immigrant-serving organization if they know of a low-cost or free health care facility in your area.

The U.S. Department of Health and Human Services funds health care facilities in many locations across the country that provide basic health care to immigrants. To find a doctor near you, visit **http://findahealthcenter.hrsa.gov**.

Federal and State Health Programs

Medicare: Medicare is a health insurance program for people who are 65 years old or older, under age 65 with certain disabilities, or have end-stage renal disease. Medicare pays for primary care and certain services if you are sick or injured. For more information about how to enroll in Medicare, visit **www.medicare.gov/MedicareEligibility/home.asp**.

Medicare has several parts, including Part A, Part B, and Part D.

- Part A is hospital insurance that helps cover inpatient care in hospitals, skilled nursing facilities, hospice, and home health care. Most people do not pay a Part A premium because they paid Medicare taxes while working. If you are not eligible for premium-free Part A, you may be able to buy Part A if you meet certain conditions.

- Part B is medical insurance that helps cover services, such as doctors' services, outpatient care, durable medical equipment, home health services, and other medical services as well as some preventive services. For Part B, you pay a monthly premium.

- Part D is prescription drug coverage that helps cover the costs of certain medications doctors prescribe for treatment. Enrolling in a Medicare Part D plan is voluntary, and you pay an additional monthly premium for this coverage.

Permanent residents can get Medicare Part A, Part B, and Part D if they meet certain conditions. Permanent residents who are 65 years old or older are automatically enrolled in Medicare Part A when they start getting Social Security retirement benefits. If you are not 65 but are eligible for other reasons, call the Social Security office near you for information about enrolling. Generally, you must have worked in the United States for 10 years (or 40 quarters) over the course of your life to receive these Part A Medicare benefits without paying a premium. For more information about Medicare and to download *Medicare & You*—the official U.S. government Medicare handbook—visit **www.medicare.gov**. Information is also available in Spanish.

Medicaid: Medicaid is a joint federal-state program for low-income residents. Each state has its own Medicaid guidelines. Medicaid pays for certain medical services, such as visits to the doctor, prescription drugs, and hospitalization. Permanent residents who entered the United States *before* August 22, 1996, may be able to receive Medicaid if they meet certain conditions. Most permanent residents who entered the United States on or after August 22, 1996, may be able to get Medicaid benefits if they have lived in the United States for five years or longer and meet certain conditions. For more information about Medicaid services in your state, visit **www.medicaid.gov**.

Children's Health Insurance Program (CHIP): Your children may be able to get free or low-cost health care through a state CHIP if they meet certain conditions. If your income is too high to qualify for Medicaid, some states have a health insurance program for infants, children, and teenagers. This insurance pays for doctor visits, prescription medicines, hospital care, and other health care services. In most states, children ages 18 and younger without health insurance and whose families meet certain income limits are eligible. Children can receive free or low-cost health care without affecting their parents' immigration status.

More Information about Medicaid and CHIP

Each state has its own Medicaid and CHIP rules, so it is important to find out about the program in your state. For information, call 1-877-543-7669 or visit **www.insurekidsnow.gov**.

Other Federal Benefits Programs

You or members of your family may be eligible for other federal benefits, depending on your immigration status, length of time in the United States, and income level. To learn more about what services might be available to you, visit **www.benefits.gov**.

Supplemental Nutrition Assistance Program (SNAP)

Some immigrants, including children, may be eligible for the Supplemental Nutrition Assistance Program (SNAP). SNAP provides you with funds to help you buy food at grocery stores. Some states have their own state-funded food assistance programs with different rules for immigrant eligibility that may vary from state to state. For information about SNAP and the eligibility requirements, visit **www.fns.usda.gov/snap**. Information about SNAP is available in 36 different languages at **www.fns.usda.gov/documents-available-other-languages**.

Services for Survivors of Domestic Violence

Immigrants and their children who are survivors of domestic violence may be eligible for federal benefits and services, such as housing at battered women's shelters or SNAP. For more information about these services, visit **www.womenshealth.gov/violence-against-women**.

Temporary Assistance for Needy Families (TANF)

Temporary Assistance for Needy Families is a federal program that provides assistance and work opportunities for qualified low-income families. Programs differ by state, and some states have their own state-funded assistance program. For more information and eligibility requirements, visit **www.acf.hhs.gov/programs/ofa/programs/tanf**.

Assistance for Disabled Immigrants

Immigrants with disabilities may be eligible for Medicaid, SNAP, and Supplemental Security Income. For information about Supplemental Security Income, visit **www.socialsecurity.gov/ssi**.

One-Stop Career Centers

The federal government funds career centers that offer training referrals, career counseling, job listings, and other employment-related services. ESL classes and job skills training are also offered to immigrants at some of these centers.

To find a One-Stop Career Center near you, visit **www.careeronestop.org** or **www.doleta.gov**.

Keeping Your Home and Family Safe

Emergencies are unexpected events that can cause harm to people and property. Emergencies can happen to anyone at any time. This section tells you how you can prepare for emergencies and how to get help when they happen.

Be Prepared

Prepare for emergencies before they happen. For information on how to prepare for an emergency, visit **www.ready.gov**. This comprehensive website provides information on how to get ready for an emergency so that you can keep your home and family safe.

Here are some things you can do to prepare:

- Be sure your doors have good locks and keep them locked at all times. Do not give your house keys to strangers. If a stranger knocks on your door, ask who they are and what they want before opening the door.

- Smoke alarms make a loud noise when there is smoke in your house or apartment. Make sure you have smoke alarms on the ceiling near bedrooms and on each level of your house. Check the alarm each month to make sure it works. Replace the batteries in your smoke alarms at least once a year.

- Find out where the nearest hospital and police and fire stations are located. Keep all important phone numbers near your phone where you can easily find them in the event of an emergency.

- Find out where the main valves for gas, electricity, and water are in your home. Be sure you know how to turn them off by hand. If you do not know how to find them, ask your landlord, local utility company, or neighbors.

- Prepare a disaster kit that includes a flashlight, portable radio, extra batteries, blankets, first-aid supplies, and enough canned or packaged food and bottled water to last for at least three days. Be sure to include trash bags, toilet paper, and pet food, if needed. Keep all of these things in one place where it is easy to find them.

- Practice with your family how to get out of your house in case of a fire or other emergency. Make sure your children know what the smoke alarm sounds like and what to do if they hear it. Plan a place to meet your family if you have to leave your home. Choose one spot outside of your home to meet and another spot outside of your neighborhood, in case you cannot return home. Ask a friend or family member living in another area to be the main person your family will call if you are separated in an emergency. Make sure everyone knows to call this person and has his or her phone number.

- Ask about emergency plans at your child's school. Make sure your child knows what to do in the event of an emergency and where you can meet him or her. Your child should know your phone number and address.

What You Can Do

To help keep your neighborhood safe, get to know your neighbors. Talk with them about how to handle an emergency in your area. If you have neighbors with disabilities, see if they will need special help in the event of an emergency.

Many neighborhoods have a Neighborhood Watch, which teaches residents how to help themselves by identifying and reporting suspicious activity in their neighborhoods. If there is a Neighborhood Watch in your area, you can volunteer to participate. If you want to start a Neighborhood Watch, call your local police department. For more information, visit **www.nnw.org**.

You help your community and nation when you help others stay safe. You can get more involved in your community through your local Citizen Corps Council. For more information, visit **www.citizencorps.gov**.

First Aid

Learn how to help in certain emergency situations, such as when someone is bleeding or choking. This is called first aid. You can take a first-aid training class through your local Red Cross. Call your local Red Cross office or the National Safety Council to ask about classes in your area. For more information, visit **www.redcross.org** or **www.nsc.org/learn/Safety-Training/Pages/first-aid-training.aspx**.

Keep a first-aid kit at home, at work, and in your car. A first-aid kit has items you can use for small injuries or for pain, such as bandages, antiseptic wipes, medicine, instant ice packs, and gloves. You can buy a first aid kit at your local drugstore.

Poison Control

Many things in your home can be poisonous if they are ingested. These can include cleaning products, medicine, paint, alcohol, cosmetics, and even some plants. Keep these things away from young children.

If someone swallows a poisonous substance, call the Poison Control Center immediately at 1-800-222-1222. You can get help 24 hours a day, seven days a week. Have the poisonous substance with you when you call so you can tell the operator what it is. If you do not speak English, tell the operator so an interpreter can help you. Calls to the Poison Control Center are confidential and free.

Stay Informed

The Department of Homeland Security (DHS) recognizes that everyone shares a responsibility for the nation's security and should be aware of the heightened risk of a terrorist attack in the United States. DHS has a system to help people understand the risk of a terrorist attack or any other threat to the nation's security. This system is called The National Terrorism Advisory System (NTAS).

NTAS alerts are issued when there is credible information that there is a threat to the nation's security. The two types of alerts are:

- **Imminent Threat Alert:** This alert warns of a credible, specific, and impending terrorist threat against the United States.

- **Elevated Threat Alert:** This alert warns of a credible terrorist threat against the United States.

For more information, visit **www.dhs.gov/alerts**.

If you would like to receive mobile updates, visit **www.twitter.com/ NTASAlerts**.

The U.S. government can use the NTAS to provide information to the public in the event of an emergency. The Secretary of Homeland Security can use this system to provide immediate information to the public when a terrorist attack occurs. State and local governments may also use the NTAS to provide emergency information to the public.

TIP If a terrorist attack, natural disaster, or other emergency occurs, listen to what local authorities tell you to do. Listen to the radio or television for instructions. Have a television or radio in your home that works on batteries in case electricity in your area is temporarily lost.

Respond to an Emergency

Emergency Help by Phone

In the United States, 911 is a number you can call on any telephone to get emergency help. 911 should only be used in the event of an emergency. Teach your family about when it is and is not appropriate to call 911. Examples are listed below.

Call 911 to:

- Report a fire;

- Report a crime in progress;

- Request emergency medical help;

- Report a gas leak; and

- Report suspicious activities, such as screams, calls for help, or gunshots.

Do <u>Not</u> Call 911 to:

- Ask for directions;

- Ask for information about public services;

- Find out if someone is in jail;

- Report situations that are not emergencies;

- Ask for information about animal control; or

- Talk to a police officer.

Call 911 for serious, life-threatening emergencies only. Calling 911 for the wrong reason may keep someone else from getting the help he or she needs. If you have a question for the police, call the non-emergency number for the police department listed in your phone book.

What Happens When I Call 911?

- Calls to 911 are usually answered within 12 seconds. You may be put on hold. When the operator answers, there will be silence on the phone for several seconds. Do not hang up. Wait for the operator to speak.

- If you do not speak English, tell the operator what language you speak. An interpreter should come on the line.

- The 911 operator will ask you questions to find out what and where the emergency is. Keep calm and answer these questions. Try to stay on the phone with the operator until you answer all questions.

Law Enforcement in the United States

In the United States, there are federal, state, and local law enforcement agencies that protect the public. In your community, law enforcement officers are the police or sheriff. Find out the phone number of the police station nearest you and keep it next to your telephone. Remember that police officers are there to protect you and your family from harm. Do not be afraid to report a crime, especially if you are the victim. Some criminals take advantage of immigrants because they think you will not report the crime to the police. If you are stopped by a police officer:

- Do not be afraid.

- Be polite and cooperative.

- Tell the officer if you do not speak English.

- If you are in a car, do not get out of the car until the officer tells you to do so.

- Keep your hands where the officer can see them. Do not reach into your pockets or into other areas of the car.

Natural Disaster Assistance

Natural disasters can strike anytime and anywhere. Natural disasters come in many forms, such as tornadoes, hurricanes, floods, or earthquakes. In the event you are affected by a natural disaster, access disaster help and resources at **www. disasterassistance.gov** or by calling 1-800-621- FEMA (3362) or 1-800-462-7585 (for hearing impaired).

If You See Something, Say Something™

Federal and state officials ask all people living in the United States to help fight terrorism. Be aware of your surroundings, especially when you travel on public buses, trains, and airplanes. If you see a suspicious item that has been left behind, such as a briefcase, backpack, or paper bag, report it immediately to the nearest police officer or other authority. Do not open or remove the item yourself. For more information, visit **www.dhs.gov**.

Learning About the United States

The United States is a representative democracy, and citizens play a very important role in governing the country. In this section, you will learn about how citizens shape the U.S. government, how the United States was founded and grew, and how our government operates.

We the People: The Role of the Citizen in the United States

In the United States, the government gets its power to govern from the people. We have a government of the people, by the people, and for the people. Citizens in the United States shape their government and its policies, so they must learn about important public issues and get involved in their communities. U.S. citizens vote in free elections to choose important government officials, such as the president, vice president, senators, and representatives. Constituents can call their elected officials to express an opinion, ask for information, or get help with specific issues.

Our government is based on several important values: freedom, opportunity, equality, and justice. Americans share these values, and these values give us a common civic identity.

Government in the United States protects the rights of each person. The United States is made up of people from different backgrounds, cultures, and religions. Our government and laws are organized so that citizens from different backgrounds and with different beliefs all have the same rights. No one can be punished or harmed for having an opinion or belief that is different from that of other people.

Of, By, and For the People: What Is Democracy?

The word "democracy" means "government by the people." Democracy can have different forms in different countries. In the United States, we have what is called a representative democracy. This means that the people choose officials to represent their views and concerns in the government.

How the United States Began

The early colonists and settlers who came to the United States were often fleeing unfair treatment, especially religious persecution, in their home countries. They were seeking freedom and new opportunities. Today, many people come to the United States for these same reasons.

Before it became a separate and independent nation, the United States was made up of 13 colonies that were ruled by Great Britain. People living in the colonies had no say in which laws were passed or how they were governed. They especially objected to taxation without representation. This means that people had to pay taxes, but they had no say in how their government operated.

By 1776, many people believed that this policy was unfair and that they should govern themselves. Representatives from the colonies issued a Declaration of Independence. This important document declared that the colonies were free, independent, and no longer ruled by Great Britain. Thomas Jefferson wrote the Declaration of Independence. He later became the third president of the United States.

The Declaration of Independence was adopted on July 4, 1776. Americans celebrate July 4 every year as Independence Day because it is our nation's birthday.

The United States had to fight for its freedom from Great Britain in the Revolutionary War. General George Washington led the Continental Army in the American Revolution. He is known as the "Father of Our Country." Later, he became the first president of the United States.

After the colonies won the war, they became states. Each state had its own government. The people in these states wanted to create a new form of government to unite the states into a single nation. Today, this central government, our national government, is called the federal government. The United States now consists of 50 states; the District of Columbia (a special area that is the home of the federal government); the territories of Guam, American Samoa, and the U.S. Virgin Islands; and the Commonwealths of the Northern Mariana Islands and Puerto Rico.

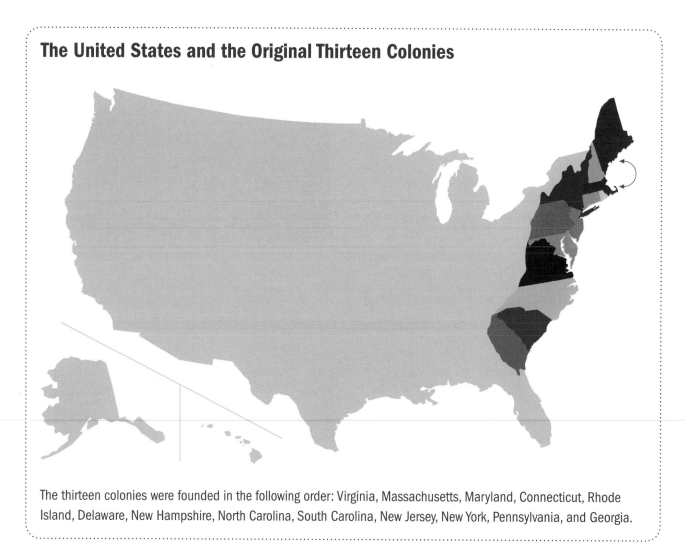

The United States and the Original Thirteen Colonies

The thirteen colonies were founded in the following order: Virginia, Massachusetts, Maryland, Connecticut, Rhode Island, Delaware, New Hampshire, North Carolina, South Carolina, New Jersey, New York, Pennsylvania, and Georgia.

Creating "A More Perfect Union"

For several years after the American Revolution, the states tried different ways to join together in a central government, but this government was too weak. In 1787, the representatives from each state gathered in Philadelphia, Pennsylvania, to develop a new, stronger central government. This meeting was called the Constitutional Convention. After much debate, leaders from the states drafted a document describing the new government. This document was called the United States Constitution. The Constitution described how the new government would be organized, how government officials would be chosen, and what rights the new central government would guarantee to citizens. Today, the Constitution remains one of the most important documents in American history.

The United States Flag

The United States flag has changed over our history. Now it has 13 stripes to represent the original 13 American colonies. It has 50 stars, one for each state. The American national anthem, called "The Star-Spangled Banner," was written about the flag. The flag is also called "Old Glory" or "Stars and Stripes."

The members of the Constitutional Convention signed the Constitution on September 17, 1787, and then all 13 states had to approve it. Some people believed that the Constitution did not do enough to protect the rights of individuals. The states agreed to approve the Constitution if a list of individual rights were added to it. The states approved the Constitution in 1788 and it went into effect in 1789. Changes to the Constitution are called amendments. The first 10 amendments to the Constitution were added in 1791. These first 10 amendments list individual rights. They are called the Bill of Rights.

The United States is a nation governed by laws. Government officials make decisions based on those laws. The Constitution is known as the supreme law of the land because every citizen, including all government officials, and every new law must uphold its principles. Laws apply equally to everyone. The federal government has limited powers. Powers not given directly to the federal government by the Constitution are held by the states.

"We the People"

"We the People" are the first three words of the United States Constitution. The Constitution begins by explaining why it was written and what it intended to accomplish. This section is called the preamble. The preamble to the Constitution reads:

"We the People of the United States, in Order to form a more perfect Union, establish Justice, insure domestic Tranquility, provide for the common defense, promote the general Welfare, and secure the Blessings of Liberty to ourselves and our Posterity, do ordain and establish this Constitution for the United States of America."

The Bill of Rights: The First 10 Amendments

The first changes to the Constitution were made to protect individual citizens and to limit the power of government. The Bill of Rights lists important individual freedoms that are promised to the American people. Some of these rights include:

- **Freedom of Speech:** You are free to think and speak as you want.

- **Freedom of Religion:** You are free to practice any religion or not practice a religion.

- **Freedom of the Press:** The government cannot decide what is printed or reported in the media.

- **Freedom to Gather or Assemble in Public Places:** You are free to meet with other people in a peaceful way.

- **Freedom to Protest Government Actions and Demand Change:** You are free to challenge government actions with which you do not agree.

In most cases, the Bill of Rights protects your right to bear arms. The Bill of Rights also guarantees due process. Due process is a set of specific legal procedures that must be followed if you are accused of a crime. Police officers and soldiers cannot stop and search you without a valid reason, and they cannot search your home without permission from a court. If you are accused of a crime, you are guaranteed a speedy trial by a jury made up of people like you. You are guaranteed legal representation and can call witnesses to speak for you. You are also protected from cruel and unusual punishment.

Changing the Constitution

The United States Constitution is called a living document because the American people, acting through their state and national representatives, can change it when necessary. These changes are called amendments. It is a long and difficult process to amend the Constitution, and it has only been amended 27 times. Besides the Bill of Rights, some important amendments are the Thirteenth, which forbids slavery; the Fourteenth, which guarantees all citizens equal protection under the law; and the Nineteenth, which gives women the right to vote.

How the Federal Government Works

The original 13 colonies had lived under the total power of the British king. In their new central government, Americans wanted to prevent a concentration of power in one government official or one office. The Constitution created three branches for the federal government so that power would be balanced. The three branches have separate responsibilities. We call this the system of checks and balances. This means that no single branch of government can become too powerful because it is balanced by the other two branches.

The Federal Government

The three branches of the federal government are:

The Legislative Branch
the United States Congress and related offices

The Executive Branch
the president, vice president, and departments of the federal government

The Judicial Branch
the Supreme Court of the United States and federal courts across the country

The Legislative Branch: Congress

Citizens of the United States vote in free elections to choose people to represent them in the United States Congress. Congress has the responsibility of making the laws for our nation. Congress is made up of the House of Representatives and the Senate.

The United States House of Representatives

People in each state vote to choose members of the House of Representatives. There are 435 voting members of the House of Representatives, which is often called "the House." The number of representatives from each state depends on how many people live in that state. States are divided into districts. People living in each district vote for someone to represent their district in the House. Each representative serves for two years, and then people have another chance to vote for their representative to remain in office or for a different person to represent them. Representatives can serve in Congress for an unlimited period of time.

There are five additional delegates in the House; these are the representatives of the District of Columbia, the Commonwealth of the Mariana Islands, and the territories of Guam, American Samoa, and the U.S. Virgin Islands. A resident commissioner represents Puerto Rico.

The House of Representatives makes laws, and it has some special responsibilities. Only the House of Representatives can:

- Propose laws about taxes.

- Decide if a government official accused of committing a crime against the country should be put on trial in the Senate. This is called impeachment.

The United States Senate

There are 100 senators in the Senate. People in each state vote to choose two senators to represent them in Congress. Senators serve for six years, and then people have another chance to re-elect those senators or to vote for a different person to represent them. Senators can serve in Congress for an unlimited period of time. Senators make laws, but they also have special responsibilities.

Only the Senate can:

- Say yes or no to any agreements the president makes with other countries or organizations of countries. These are called treaties.

- Approve or not approve individuals the president chooses for high-level jobs, such as Supreme Court justices or officials to run federal departments, such as the Department of Education or the Department of Health and Human Services.

- Hold a trial for a government official who has been impeached by the House of Representatives.

Government Officials Serve the People

In the United States, everyone can contact their elected representative and senators. Visit **www.house.gov** or **www.senate.gov** to identify your representative or senator. You can call 202-224-3121 and ask for your representative's or senators' offices. This is not a free call. You can write to your representative or senators to ask questions or to give your opinion about legislation and the federal government, or if you have a problem and need help with federal benefits.

To write to your representative:

The Honorable (add representative's full name)
U.S. House of Representatives
Washington, DC 20515

To write to your senator:

The Honorable (add senator's full name)
United States Senate
Washington, DC 20510

You can visit the websites of Congress to learn about current activities in the House and Senate and about your own representative and senators, including their website addresses.

- For the House of Representatives, visit **www.house.gov**.

- For the Senate, visit **www.senate.gov**.

The Executive Branch: The President

The president is the leader of the executive branch and is responsible for upholding and enforcing the laws of the country. The president has many other responsibilities, such as setting national policies, proposing laws to Congress, and choosing high-level officials and members of the Supreme Court. The president also is the leader of the United States military and is called the commander in chief.

People vote in elections for the president and vice president every four years. The president can only serve in office for two four-year terms. The vice president becomes president if the president dies, resigns, or can no longer work.

You can learn about the president by visiting the website for the White House, the president's home and office, at **www.whitehouse.gov**.

The Judicial Branch: The Supreme Court

The Constitution created the Supreme Court, the highest court in the United States. There are nine judges on the Supreme Court. They are called justices. The president chooses the justices of the Supreme Court, and they serve as long as they are able. The Supreme Court can overrule both state and federal laws if they conflict with the Constitution. There are also other federal courts, such as the U.S. District Courts and the U.S. Circuit Courts of Appeals.

To learn more about the Supreme Court of the United States, visit **www.supremecourt.gov**.

State and Local Government

In addition to the federal government, each state has its own constitution and government. Each state government also has three branches: legislative, executive, and judicial.

The leader of the state executive branch is called the governor. The people of each state vote in elections to choose their governor and their representatives to the state legislature. The state legislature makes the laws that apply in each state. These laws cannot go against the U.S. Constitution. Each state judicial branch upholds the laws of that state.

Each state also has local governments. There are city or county governments, or sometimes both. They provide and oversee many services in your local community, such as public schools, libraries, police and fire departments, and water, gas, and electric services. People in local communities usually vote for local government officials, but some local officials are appointed. Local governments have different forms. Some have mayors as their leaders; others have city or county councils. Local communities also have school boards, a group of citizens who are elected or appointed to oversee the public schools.

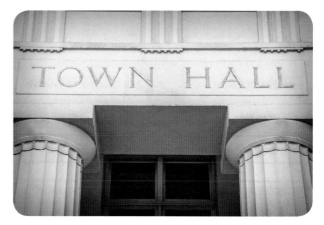

What You Can Do

Many local government meetings are open to the public and are held at night so that anyone can attend. For example, you can go to a city council meeting or a school board meeting to learn more about what is going on in your community. The meeting times and locations are usually listed in the local newspaper or on the local government's website. Some local government meetings are broadcast on the local cable television channel.

Experience the United States

You can learn more about the United States by visiting our national parks, which include some of our nation's most majestic and historic sites. You can experience your America in national parks such as:

- Yellowstone National Park, with the world's largest collection of geysers, including Old Faithful.

- Independence National Historical Park, home to Independence Hall and the Liberty Bell.

- Mammoth Cave National Park, which contains the longest cave system in the world.

- Denali National Park and Preserve, home to North America's tallest mountain, Mount McKinley.

The National Park System includes more than 400 national monuments, battlefields, historic sites, seashores, and more. National parks are located in every state, the District of Columbia, and five U.S. territories.

To learn more about our national parks, visit the National Park Service website at **www.nps.gov**.

Becoming a U.S. Citizen

Becoming a U.S. citizen gives permanent residents new rights and privileges. Citizenship also brings with it new responsibilities. This section discusses reasons to consider U.S. citizenship and describes what you need to do to become a citizen.

Why Become a U.S. Citizen?

To become a citizen, you must be willing to:

- Swear your loyalty to the United States;

- Give up your allegiance to any other country; and

- Support and defend the United States and its Constitution.

When you become a citizen, you accept all of the responsibilities of being an American. In return, you get certain rights and privileges. Permanent residents have most of the rights of U.S. citizens, but there are many important reasons to consider becoming a U.S. citizen, such as:

- **Voting:** Only citizens can vote in federal elections. In most states, only U.S. citizens are allowed to vote in elections.

- **Serving on a Jury:** Only U.S. citizens can serve on a federal jury. In most states, only U.S. citizens are allowed to serve on a jury. Serving on a jury is an important responsibility for U.S. citizens.

- **Traveling with a U.S. Passport:** A U.S. passport enables U.S. citizens to get assistance from the U.S. government when overseas, if necessary.

- **Bringing Family Members to the United States:** Generally, U.S. citizens get priority when petitioning to bring family members permanently to this country.

- **Obtaining Citizenship for Children Born Abroad:** In most cases, a child born abroad to a U.S. citizen is automatically a U.S. citizen.

- **Becoming Eligible for Federal Jobs:** Certain jobs with government agencies require U.S. citizenship.

- **Becoming an Elected Official:** Only citizens can run for federal office and for most state and local offices.

- **Keeping Your Residency:** A U.S. citizen's right to remain in the United States cannot be taken away.

- **Becoming Eligible for Federal Grants and Scholarships:** Many financial aid grants, including college scholarships and funds given by the government for specific purposes, are available only to U.S. citizens.

- **Obtaining Government Benefits:** Some government benefits are available only to U.S. citizens.

Getting Naturalization Information

People 18 years old or older who want to become citizens should get Form M-476, A Guide to Naturalization. This guide has important information on the requirements for naturalization. It also describes the forms you will need to begin the naturalization process.

To see if you are eligible to apply for naturalization, visit the Citizenship Resource Center at **www.uscis.gov/citizenship**. Use Form N-400, Application for Naturalization, to apply for naturalization. There is a fee to file Form N-400. To check the fee for filing Form N-400 or any USCIS form, visit **www.uscis.gov/fees**.

To get Forms M-476 and N-400, call the USCIS Forms Line at 1-800-870-3676 or get them from **www.uscis.gov**.

For more specific information about USCIS policies and naturalization eligibility requirements, review the USCIS Policy Manual at **www.uscis.gov/policymanual**. The Policy Manual is USCIS' centralized online repository for immigration policies.

Naturalization: Becoming a U.S. Citizen

The process of becoming a U.S. citizen is called naturalization. In general, you can apply for naturalization once you meet the following requirements:

Requirements for Naturalization

1. Continuous residence: Live in the United States as a permanent resident for a specific amount of time.

2. Physical presence: Show that you have been physically present in the United States for specific time periods.

3. Time in state or USCIS district: Show that you have lived in your state or USCIS district for a specific amount of time.

4. Good moral character: Show that you have behaved in a legal and acceptable manner.

5. English and civics: Know basic English and information about U.S. history and government.

6. Attachment to the Constitution: Understand and accept the principles of the U.S. Constitution.

You may qualify for certain exceptions and modifications if:

- You are a U.S. national;

- You are employed abroad in a qualifying category;

- You have qualifying military service; or

- You are the spouse, child, or parent of certain U.S. citizens.

Consult Form M-476, A Guide to Naturalization, for more information at **www.uscis.gov/natzguide**. You may also wish to consult an immigration attorney or BIA-accredited representative. See page 21 for more information.

1. Continuous Residence

Continuous residence means that you must live in the United States as a permanent resident for a certain period of time. Most people must be permanent residents in continuous residence for five years (or three years if married to a U.S. citizen) before they can begin the naturalization process.

The date you became a permanent resident (usually the date on your Permanent Resident Card) is the date your five years begins. If you leave the United States for a long period of time, usually six months or more, you may break your continuous residence.

If you leave the United States for one year or longer, you may be able to return if you have a re-entry permit. You should apply for this re-entry permit before you depart the United States. See page 17 for information on how to apply for a re-entry permit. In most cases, none of the time you were in the United States before you left the country will count toward your time in continuous residence. This means that you will need to begin your continuous residence again **after** you return to the United States, and you may have to wait up to four years and one day before you can apply for naturalization.

Additionally, if you must leave the United States for certain employment purposes, you may need to file Form N-470, Application to Preserve Residence for Naturalization Purposes, in order to preserve your status as a permanent resident in order to pursue naturalization.

Be aware that absences from the United States while your naturalization application is pending could cause problems with your eligibility, especially if you accept employment abroad.

MAINTAINING CONTINUOUS RESIDENCE AS A PERMANENT RESIDENT		
If you leave the United States for:	**Your residence status is:**	**To keep your status you must:**
More than six months	Possibly broken	Prove that you continued to live, work, and/or have ties to the United States (for example, paid taxes) while you were away.
More than one year	Broken	In most cases, you must begin your continuous residence over. Apply for a re-entry permit before you leave if you plan to return to the United States as a permanent resident. You may also need to file Form N-470, Application to Preserve Residence for Naturalization Purposes.

Preserving Your Residence for Naturalization Purposes: Exemptions for One-Year Absences

If you work for the U.S. government, a recognized U.S. research institution, or certain U.S. corporations, or if you are a member of the clergy serving abroad, you may be able to preserve your continuous residence if you:

1. Have been physically present and living in the United States without leaving for at least one year after becoming a permanent resident.

2. Submit Form N-470, Application to Preserve Residence for Naturalization Purposes, before you have been outside the United States for one year. There is a fee to file Form N-470. To check the filing fee for Form N-470 or any USCIS form, visit **www.uscis.gov/fees**.

For more information, contact the USCIS Forms Line at 1-800-870-3676 and ask for Form N-470. You can also get the form on the USCIS website at **www.uscis.gov**.

TIP

A re-entry permit (Form I-131, Application for Travel Document) and Form N-470, Application to Preserve Residence for Naturalization Purposes, are not the same. You may show a re-entry permit instead of your Permanent Resident Card (if you have been gone for less than 12 months) or instead of a visa (if you have been gone for more than 12 months) when you want to re-enter the United States after a temporary absence. However, if you wish to apply for naturalization and have been absent for more than 12 months, you may need to also file Form N-470 in order to preserve your residence for naturalization purposes.

Exemptions for Military Personnel

If you are on active duty status or were recently discharged from the U.S. armed forces, the continuous residence and physical presence requirements may not apply to you. You can find more information in Form M-599, Naturalization Information for Military Personnel. Every military base should have a point-of-contact to handle your naturalization application and certify a Form N-426, Request for Certification of Military or Naval Service. You must submit Form N-426 with your application forms. To get the forms you need, call the USCIS Military Help Line at 1-877-CIS-4MIL (1-877-247-4645). You can find more information at **www.uscis.gov/military** or by calling Customer Service at 1-800-375-5283.

2. Physical Presence

Physical presence means that you actually have been present in the United States. If you are a permanent resident, you must be physically present in the United States for at least 30 months during the last five years (or 18 months during the last three years, if married to a U.S. citizen) before you apply for naturalization.

The Difference between Physical Presence and Continuous Residence

Physical presence is the total days you were inside the United States and does not include the time you spend outside the United States. Each day you spend outside the United States takes away from your physical presence total. If you are away from the United States for long periods of time or if you take many short trips outside the country, you may not meet your physical presence requirement. To count your physical presence time, you should add together all the time you have been in the United States. Then subtract all trips you have taken outside the United States. This even includes short trips to Canada and Mexico. For example, if you go to Mexico for a weekend, you must include the trip when counting how many days you spent out of the country.

Continuous residence is the total time you have resided as a permanent resident in the United States before applying for naturalization. If you spend too much time outside the United States during a single trip, you may break your continuous residence.

3. Time in State or USCIS District

Most people must live in the state or USCIS district where they apply for naturalization for at least three months. Students can apply for naturalization either where they go to school or where their family lives (if they depend on their parents for support).

4. Good Moral Character

To be eligible for naturalization, you must be a person of good moral character. A person is not considered to be of good moral character if he or she commits certain crimes during the five years before applying for naturalization, or if he or she does not tell the truth during the naturalization interview.

Behaviors That Might Show a Lack of Good Moral Character

- Drunk driving or being drunk on a regular basis

- Illegal gambling

- Prostitution

- Lying to gain immigration benefits

- Failing to pay court-ordered child support or alimony

- Persecuting someone because of race, religion, national origin, political opinion, or social group

If you commit some specific crimes, you can never become a U.S. citizen and will probably be removed from the country. These crimes are called bars to naturalization. Crimes called aggravated felonies (if committed on or after November 29, 1990), including: murder; rape; sexual abuse of a child; violent assault; treason; and illegal trafficking in drugs, firearms, or people are some examples of permanent bars to naturalization. In most cases, immigrants who were exempted or discharged from serving in the U.S. armed forces because they were immigrants and immigrants who deserted from the U.S. armed forces are also permanently barred from U.S. citizenship.

You also may be denied citizenship if you behave in other ways that show you lack good moral character.

Other crimes are temporary bars to naturalization. Temporary bars usually prevent you from becoming a citizen for up to five years after you commit the crime. These include:

- Any crime against a person with intent to harm;

- Any crime against property or the government involving fraud;

- Two or more crimes with combined sentences of five years or more;

- Violating controlled substance laws (for example, using or selling illegal drugs); and

- Spending 180 days or more during the past five years in jail or prison.

Report any crimes that you committed when you apply for naturalization. This includes crimes removed from your record or committed before your 18th birthday. If you do not tell USCIS about them, you may be denied citizenship and you could be prosecuted.

5. English and Civics

In general, you must show that you can understand, read, write, and speak basic English. You must also have a basic knowledge of U.S. history and government (also known as civics). You are required to pass an English and a civics test to prove your knowledge.

Many schools and community organizations help people prepare for their citizenship tests. You can find test questions at **www.uscis.gov/citizenship** and **www.uscis.gov/teststudymaterials**. USCIS offers a variety of free study materials, such as booklets, flash cards, practice tests, and videos. You can get information about citizenship and English classes at **www.uscis.gov/citizenship**.

6. Attachment to the Constitution

You must be willing to support and defend the United States and its Constitution. You declare your attachment or loyalty to the United States and the Constitution when you take the *Oath of Allegiance*. You become a U.S. citizen when you take the *Oath of Allegiance*.

In certain circumstances, there can be a modification of the *Oath of Allegiance*. If you show that you have a physical or developmental disability that makes you unable to understand the meaning of the *Oath*, it can be waived.

If you have a pending naturalization application and you move, you must notify USCIS of your new address. File Form AR-11, Change of Address, within 10 days of your relocation. For more information or to change your address online, visit **www.uscis.gov/addresschange** or call Customer Service at 1-800-375-5283. You must notify USCIS **each time** you change your address.

Exemptions, Exceptions, and Accommodations

English Language and Civics Exemptions

Some people who apply for naturalization have different test requirements because of their age and the length of time they have lived in the United States.

EXEMPTIONS TO THE ENGLISH AND CIVICS REQUIREMENTS

If you are:	Lived as permanent resident in the United States for:	You do not take the:	You must take the:
Age 50 or older	20 years	English test	Civics test in your language
Age 55 or older	15 years	English test	Civics test in your language
Age 65 or older	20 years	English test	Simplified civics test in your language

If you do not have to take the English test, you must bring your own translator for the civics test.

Medical Exceptions

If you have a physical or developmental disability or mental impairment(s), you can seek an exception for the English and/or civics requirements. To get more information, contact the USCIS Forms Line at 1-800-870-3676 and ask for Form N-648, Medical Certification for Disability Exceptions, or get a copy from the USCIS website at **www.uscis.gov/n-648**.

Disability Accommodations

USCIS makes every reasonable effort to help applicants with disabilities complete the naturalization process. For example, if you use a wheelchair, USCIS will make sure that you can be fingerprinted, interviewed, and naturalized at a location that is wheelchair accessible. If you are deaf or hearing impaired and need a sign language interpreter, USCIS will make arrangements with you to have one at your interview. If you need an accommodation due to a disability, please call Customer Service at 1-800-375-5283 or 1-800-767-1833 (for hearing impaired) to request an accommodation.

Naturalization Ceremonies

If USCIS approves your application for naturalization, you must attend a ceremony and take the *Oath of Allegiance*. USCIS will send you Form N-445, Notice of Naturalization Oath Ceremony, to tell you the time and date of your ceremony. You must complete this form and bring it to your ceremony.

If you cannot go to your ceremony, you can reschedule your ceremony. To reschedule, you must return Form N-445 to your local USCIS office along with a letter explaining why you cannot attend the ceremony.

You will return your Permanent Resident Card to USCIS when you check in at the ceremony. You will no longer need your card because you will get a Certificate of Naturalization at the ceremony.

You are not a citizen until you have taken the *Oath of Allegiance*. An official will read each part of the *Oath* slowly and ask you to repeat the words. After you take the *Oath*, you will receive your Certificate of Naturalization. This certificate proves that you are a U.S. citizen.

The *Oath of Allegiance* ceremony is a public event. Many communities hold special ceremonies on Independence Day, July 4, of each year. Check to see if your community holds a special July 4 citizenship ceremony and how you can participate. Many people bring their families and celebrate after the ceremony.

You're on Your Way

We hope that you find this guide useful. It was written to help you as you start your life in the United States and to help you understand your rights and responsibilities as a permanent resident. The guide tells you ways that you can become involved in your community. It also tells you some of the things that you will have to learn about if you wish to become a naturalized citizen. Visit the USCIS website at **www.uscis.gov** to learn more. You will find other helpful materials at **www.welcometousa.gov**.

Now that you are here, you have a chance to experience everything that life can be in this country. We welcome you as a permanent resident, and we wish you a successful life in the United States.